Robert Smith and Co.

Amendments of the General School Laws of the Session of

Legislature

1891

Robert Smith and Co.

Amendments of the General School Laws of the Session of Legislature
1891

ISBN/EAN: 9783337232382

Printed in Europe, USA, Canada, Australia, Japan

Cover: Foto ©Suzi / pixelio.de

More available books at **www.hansebooks.com**

TO THE

General School Laws

AT THE

SESSION OF THE LEGISLATURE, 1891

COMPILED AT THE OFFICE OF THE
SUPERINTENDENT OF PUBLIC INSTRUCTION
1891

BY AUTHORITY

During the last session of the Legislature several amendments were made to the school law, and new laws were enacted in regard to the supervision of schools, the granting of teachers' certificates by the University of Michigan, the introduction of the kindergarten method into the public schools of the State, and the organization of township school districts in the Upper Peninsula. The numbers refer to the sections, chapters and pages of the compilation of 1889. It is suggested that this copy be . pasted in your copy of the school law, and that some mark be made to indicate the sections amended. A copy of this pamphlet will be furnished to any school officer or teacher on application to the Superintendent of Public Instruction, Lansing.

FERRIS S. FITCH,
Superintendent of Public Instruction.

AMENDMENTS TO SCHOOL LAWS.

CHAPTER III.—SECTION 19.

[(§ 46.) Page 21. Amended by act No. 21. Takes effect Oct. 1, 1891.]

SEC. 19. The district board may admit to the district schools non-resident pupils, and may determine the rates of tuition of such pupils and collect the same: *Provided*, That when non-resident pupils, their parents or guardians, pay a school tax in said district, the same shall be credited on their tuition a sum not to exceed the amount of such tuition and they shall only be required to pay tuition for the difference therein. *(Non-resident pupils' tuition. Proviso.)*

CHAPTER X.—SECTION 3.

[(§ 109.) Page 40. Amended by act No. 21. Takes effect Oct. 1, 1891.]

SEC. 3. It shall be the duty of the board of trustees in any graded school district: *(Duty of trustees.)*

First, To classify and grade the pupils attending schools in such district and cause them to be taught in such schools or departments as they may deem expedient; *(To classify pupils.)*

Second, To establish in such district a high school when ordered by a vote of the district at an annual meeting, and to determine the qualifications for admission to such school, and the fees to be paid for tuition in any branch taught therein: *Provided*, That when non-resident pupils, their parents or guardians, shall pay a school tax in said district, the same shall be credited on their tuition a sum not to exceed the amount of such tuition and they shall only be required to pay tuition for the difference between the amount of the tax and the amount charged for tuition; *(To establish high school, etc. Proviso as to non-resident pupils' tuition.)*

Third, To audit and order the payment of all [of] the accounts of the director for incidental or other expenses incurred by him in the discharge of his duties; but no more than fifty dollars shall be expended by the director in one year for repairs of the buildings or appurtenances of *(To audit and pay directors' accounts.)*

the district property without the authority of the board of trustees;

To employ teachers.

Fourth, To employ all qualified teachers necessary for the several schools, and to determine the amount of their compensation and to require the director and moderator to make contracts with the same on behalf of the district, in accordance with the provisions of law concerning contracts with teachers;

To employ officers, etc.

Fifth, To employ such officers and servants as may be necessary for the management of the schools and school property, and prescribe their duties and fix their compensation;

Other duties.

Sixth, To perform such other duties as are required of district boards in other school districts.

CHAPTER X.

[Page 21. Amended by act No. 84, adding a new section, to stand as section No. 6. Takes effect May 20, 1891.]

Duty of trustees in certain cases, etc.

SEC. 6. Whenever the trustees of any organized graded school district shall be presented twenty days before the annual meeting thereof, with a petition signed by ten electors of said district, stating that it is the desire of said petitioners that at the annual meeting of said school district there shall be submitted to said annual meeting the proposition to change from a graded school district to one or more primary school districts the said trustees shall, in their

In case of vote to change from graded school district to primary.

notice of such annual meeting, state that the proposition set forth in said petition will be presented to said meeting, and if two-thirds of the qualified voters present at said meeting shall vote to change to one or more primary school districts such change shall be made, and it shall be the duty of the board of school inspectors of the township or townships in which such district is situated, upon being duly notified of such vote, to proceed to change or divide such district as determined by such annual meeting, and they shall provide for the holding of the first meeting in the or each of the proposed primary school districts in the same manner as is provided for by law for the organization of primary school districts, and whenever a fractional graded school district shall be so changed, the township boards of school inspectors of the respective townships where such graded school district is situated, shall organize the said district into one or more primary school districts, as provided for by law.

[NOTE.—Page 69, second paragraph.]

Act 141 of the Public Acts of 1891 repeals Act No. 214, Public Acts of 1889 providing that, if in any city and any township or part of township adjoining thereto (the same being within one county) any money remains in the fund for payment of losses by killing of sheep by dogs "after the payment of the orders payable out of the same and the amount of said money shall exceed the sum of two hundred dollars, the sum in excess of two hundred dollars shall be apportioned by said county treasurer to the said township or part of township and said city in proportion to the amount contributed to said fund during the preceding year, and the amount so apportioned to any said township or part of township, or said city, shall be respectively apportioned among the several school districts of said township or part of township and said city, in proportion to the number of children therein of school age." The distribution of the surplus will hereafter be made in accordance with the provisions of section 6 of Act No. 198, Public Acts of 1877, as amended by Act No. 283 of the Public Acts of 1881.

[ACT No. 119.]

[Takes effect Oct. 1, 1891.]

*AN ACT authorizing the introduction of the kindergarten method in the public schools of this State.

SECTION 1. *The People of the State of Michigan enact,* That in addition to the duties imposed by law upon the district board of every school district in this State, they shall also be empowered to provide a suitable room or apartment for kindergarten work, and to supply their district respectively with the necessary apparatus and appliances for the instruction of children in what is known as the kindergarten method. *Duty of district board.*

SEC. 2. In the employment of teachers it shall be competent for such district board to require qualifications for instruction of children in kindergarten methods, and the district board may provide by contract with the teacher for such instruction, specifying the hours and times therefor under such rules as the district board may prescribe. *Qualifications of teachers, etc.*

SEC. 3. All children residing within the district between the ages of four and seven shall be entitled to instructions in the kindergarten department of such district school. *What children entitled to instruction.*

SEC. 4. The powers and duties herein imposed or conferred upon the district shall also be and the same are hereby imposed and conferred upon the school trustees or board *Act to apply to certain other schools.*

* This law permits the introduction of the kindergarten method, but does not make it mandatory.

of education or other body, by whatever name known, managing or controlling the public schools in each city and village of this State; and this act is hereby made applicable to every public school organized by special act or by charter as fully as if they were named herein.

[ACT No. 144.]

[Takes effect June 19, 1891.]

AN ACT to authorize the faculty of the department of literature, science and the arts, of the University of Michigan to give teachers' certificates in certain cases.

University may issue certificate to teach, etc.

SECTION 1. *The People of the State of Michigan enact,* That the faculty of the department of literature, science and the arts, of the University of Michigan, shall give to every person receiving a bachelor's, master's or doctor's degree, and also a teacher's diploma for work done in the science and the arts of teaching from said University, a certificate, which shall serve as a legal certificate of qualification to teach in any of the schools of this State, when a copy thereof shall have been filed or recorded in the office of the legal examining officer or officers of the county, township, city or district. Such certificate shall not be liable to be annulled except by the said faculty of the said University; but its effect may be suspended in any county, township, city or district, and the holder thereof may be stricken from the list of qualified teachers in such county, township, city or district, by the legal examining officer or officers of the said county, township, city, or district, for any cause and in the same manner that such examining officer or officers may be by law authorized to revoke certificates given by himself or themselves, and such suspension shall continue in force until revoked by the authority suspending it.

Of annulling certificate, etc.

[ACT No. 147.]

[Takes effect June 19, 1891.]

AN ACT to provide for the election of a county commissioner of schools, for the appointment of school examiners, [and] to define the duties and fix the compensation for the same, and to repeal all existing acts or parts of acts conflicting with the provisions of this act.

Election of county commissioner of schools.

SECTION 1. *The People of the State of Michigan enact,* That at the meetings of the several boards of supervisors of the different counties of the State, to be held on the fourth

Monday in June, eighteen hundred ninety-one, the said several boards of supervisors shall elect a county commissioner of schools for their respective counties, whose term of office shall commence on the fourth Tuesday of August next following, who shall hold his or her office until the first day Term of office. of July, eighteen hundred ninety-three, or until his or her successor shall be elected and qualified. Said boards of super- Appointment of school examiners. visors shall also on said fourth Monday of June, appoint two persons as school examiners, who, together with said commissioner of schools, shall constitute a board of school examiners. One of said school examiners shall be appointed Term of office for a period of one year and the other for a period of two years, from and after the second Monday of October next after their appointment, or until their successors have been appointed and have qualified; and thereafter such boards of Annual appointment of examiner. supervisors shall, at each annual session, appoint one examiner who shall hold his office for a period of two years, or until his successor shall have been appointed and qualified. Within ten days after such commissioner or examiners shall Oath of office. have received legal notice of his or her election, he or she shall take and subscribe to the constitutional oath of office and the same shall be filed with the county clerk. The said county commissioner, so appointed, shall execute a bond with Bond. two sufficient sureties, to be approved by and filed with the county clerk, in the penal sum of one thousand dollars, conditioned that he or she will faithfully discharge the duties of his or her office according to law, and to faithfully account for and pay over to the proper persons all money which may come into his or her hands by reason of his or her holding such office; and thereupon the county clerk shall report the County clerk to report address, etc. name and postoffice address of such county commissioner to the State Superintendent of Public Instruction.

SEC. 2. There shall be elected at the election held on the Biennial election of commissioner. first Monday in April, eighteen hundred ninety-three, and every second year thereafter, in each county, one county commissioner of schools, whose term of office shall commence on Term of office. the first day of July next following his or her election, and who shall continue in office two years or until his or her successor shall be elected and qualified. The county com- To file oath and bond, missioner of schools elected under the provisions of this section shall file with the county clerk for the county for which he or she is elected his or her oath of office and bond, the same as provided in section one of this act, and the county clerk shall make the same report to the Superintendent of Public Instruction in all respects as provided in section one of this act.

SEC. 3. No person shall be eligible to the office of county Eligibility to office of, etc. commissioner of schools who shall not be a graduate in the literary department of some reputable college, university or State normal school, or hold a State teacher's certificate, or who shall not have held a first grade certificate, within two years next preceding the time of his or her election, or shall

2

have held the office of county commissioner **under this act:**
Proviso as to certain counties. *Provided,* That in counties having less than **fifty schools sub-**
ject to the supervision of the county commissioner, **a person**
holding at the time of his or her election a second **grade**
certificate shall be eligible.

Board to hold regular examinations, etc. SEC. 4. The board of school examiners **shall, for the**
purpose of examining all persons who may offer **themselves**
as teachers for the public schools, hold **two regular public**
examinations in each year at the county seat, **which exam-**
inations shall begin on the first Thursday of **March and**
Special examinations. August in each year; and for a like purpose the board **of**
school examiners shall hold not to exceed four special **public**
examinations at such times and places as in the **judgment**
of the board of school examiners the interests **of the**
Proviso. schools and teachers of the county may require: *Provided,*
The first and second grade certificates shall be granted **only**
at the regular public examinations provided for in this **sec-**
Schedule of examinations. tion. It shall be the duty of the county commissioner **to**
make out a schedule of the times and places of **holding**
special examinations and to cause it to be published in **one**
or more newspapers of the county at least ten **days before**
each special examination, and he or she shall send a **copy**
thereof to the chairman of each township board of **school**
inspectors in the county at least ten days previous to **the**
time of holding any special examination.

Meeting of board to grant certificates, etc. SEC. 5. The board of school examiners shall meet on **the**
Saturday following such public examination held by **the**
county commissioner and shall grant certificates to **teachers**
in such form as the Superintendent of Public **Instruction**
shall prescribe, licensing as teachers all persons who shall **have**
attained the age of sixteen years, who have attended **said**
public examinations and who shall be found qualified **in**
respect to good moral character, learning and ability to **instruct**
and govern a school, but no certificate shall be granted **to**
any person who shall not pass a satisfactory examination **in**
orthography, reading, writing, grammar, geography, **arith-**
metic, theory and art of teaching, United States history, **civil**
government and physiology and hygiene with reference **to**
the effects of alcoholic drinks, stimulants and narcotics **upon**
Signing of certificates. the human system. All certificates shall be signed by **the**
county commissioner and by at least one other **member**
Who deemed qualified teacher. of the board of examiners. No person shall be **considered**
a qualified teacher within the meaning of this act, nor **shall**
any school officer employ or contract with any person **to**
teach in any of the public schools, under the **provisions**
of this act, who has not a certificate in force, granted **by**
the board of school examiners or other lawful **authority.**
Of examination questions. All examination questions shall be prepared and **furnished**
by the Superintendent of Public Instruction to the **county**
commissioner under seal, to be opened in the presence **of**
the applicants for certificates on the day of **examination.**
Grades of certificates. SEC. 6. There shall be three grades of certificates **granted**
by the board of school examiners, in its discretion, **and**

subject to such rules and regulations as the Superintendent of Public Instruction may prescribe, which grades of certificates shall be as follows: The certificate of the first First grade. grade shall be granted only to those who have taught at least one year with ability and success, and it shall be valid throughout the State for four years: *Provided*, That no Proviso. first grade certificate shall be valid in any county other than that in which it was granted, unless a copy of said certificate, certified by the county commissioner who issued the same shall be filed with the county commissioner in the county in which the holder of said certificate desires to teach. The certificate of [the] second grade shall be granted only Second grade. to those who shall have taught at least seven months with ability and success, and it shall be valid throughout the county for which it shall be granted for three years. The Third grade. certificate of the third grade shall license the holder thereof to teach in the county for which it shall be granted for one year: *Provided*, That the county commissioner shall have Proviso. power upon personal examination satisfactory to himself or herself to grant certificates which shall license the holder thereof to teach in a specified district for which it shall be granted, but such certificate shall not continue in force beyond the time of the next public examination and it shall not in any way exempt the teacher from a full examination: *Provided further*, That in case the holder of a special cer- Further proviso. tificate does not appear for examination before the board at the next public examination succeeding the date of such special examination, a second special certificate shall not be granted to such person, except when it appears to the commissioner on good evidence that the absence was occasioned by sickness or other unavoidable cause.

SEC. 7. The board of school examiners may suspend or Suspension of certificate, etc. revoke any teacher's certificate issued by them for any reason which would have justified said board in withholding the same when given for neglect of duty, for incompetency to instruct or govern a school, or for immorality, and the said board may, within their jurisdiction, suspend for immorality or incompetency to instruct and govern a school the effect of any teacher's certificates that may have been granted by other lawful authority: *Provided*, That no certificates shall Proviso. be suspended or revoked without a personal hearing, unless the holder thereof shall, after a reasonable notice, neglect or refuse to appear before the said board for that purpose.

SEC. 8. It shall be the duty of the county commissioner: Duty of commissioner.

First, Immediately after his or her qualification as com- Notice of qualification. missioner, to send notice thereof to the Superintendent of Public Instruction and the chairman of each township board of school inspectors of the county;

Second, To keep a record of all examinations held by the Record of examinations, etc. board of school examiners and to sign all certificates and other papers and reports issued by the board;

Third, To receive the institute fees provided by law Of fees.

and to pay the same to the county treasurer quarterly, beginning September thirty, in each year;

Record of certificates.

Fourth, To keep a record of all certificates granted, suspended or revoked by the said board or commissioner, showing to whom issued, together with the date, grade, duration of each certificate and, if suspended or revoked, with the date and reason thereof;

List of teachers, etc.

Fifth, To furnish, previous to the first Monday in September in each year to the township clerk of each township in the county, a list of all persons legally authorized to teach in the county at large, and in such township, with the date and term of each certificate, and if any have been suspended or revoked, the date of such suspension ·or revocation;

To visit schools, etc.

Sixth, To visit each of the schools in the county at least once in each year and to examine carefully the discipline, the mode of instruction, and the progress and proficiency

Proviso as to assistant visitors.

of pupils: *Provided,* That in case the county commissioner is unable to visit all the schools of the county as herein required, the said commissioner may appoint such assistant visitors as may be necessary, who shall perform such duties pertaining to the visitation and supervision of schools as said commissioner shall direct: *Provided,* That the whole expense incurred by such assistant visitors shall not exceed the sum of ninety dollars in any one year;

Counsel with teachers, etc.

Seventh, To counsel with the teachers and school boards as to the courses of study to be pursued, and as to any improvement in the discipline and instruction in the schools;

Improvement of schools, etc.

Eighth, To promote by such means as he or she may devise, the improvement of the schools in the county, and the elevation of the character and qualifications of the teachers and officers thereof, and act as assistant conductor of institutes appointed by the Superintendent of Public Instruction and perform such other duties pertaining thereto as the superintendent shall require;

To receive annual reports, etc.

Ninth, To receive the duplicate annual reports of the several boards of school inspectors, examine into the correctness of the same, requiring them to be amended when necessary, indorse his or her approval upon them, and immediately thereafter and before the first day of November in each year, transmit to the Superintendent of Public Instruction one copy of each of said reports and file the other in the office of the county clerk;

Subject to instructions of Supt. Public Instruction, etc.

Tenth, To be subject to such instructions and rules as the Superintendent of Public Instruction may prescribe; to receive all blanks and communications that may be sent to him or her by the Superintendent of Public Instruction and to dispose of the same as directed by the said Superintendent, and to make annual reports at the close of the school year to the Superintendent of Public Instruction of his or her official labor, and of the schools of the county, together with such other information as may be required;

Eleventh, To perform such other duties as may be `Other duties.` required of him or her by law, and at the close of the term of office to deliver all records, books and papers belonging to the office, to his or her successor.

SEC. 9. It shall be the duty of the chairman of the `Duty of chairmen, etc.` board of school inspectors of each township:

First, To have general supervisory charge of the schools `Supervision of Schools, etc.` of his township, subject to such advice and direction as the county commissioner may give;

Second, To make such reports of his official labors and `To make reports, etc.` of the condition of the schools as the Superintendent of Public Instruction may direct or commissioner request.

SEC. 10. The compensation of each commissioner shall be `Compensation of commissioner.` determined by the board of supervisors of each county respectively, but the compensation shall not be fixed at a sum less than five hundred dollars per annum in any county where there are fifty schools under his or her supervision; at not less than one thousand dollars per annum where there are one hundred schools under such supervision; and not less than twelve hundred dollars where there are one hundred and twenty-five schools under his supervision; and in no case shall such compensation exceed the sum of fifteen hundred dollars per annum. Each mem- `Of examiners.` ber of the board of school examiners other than the county commissioner shall receive four dollars for each day actually employed in the duties of his office. The compen- `Of assistant visitors.` sation of any assistant visitor, when appointed as provided in this act, shall be determined by the county commissioner, but in no case shall it exceed three dollars for each day employed. The compensation of the county commissioner, `To be paid quarterly.` members of the board of school examiners and of any assistant visitor shall be paid quarterly from the county treasury, upon such commissioner or visitor filing with the county clerk a certified statement of/ his or her account, which shall give in separate items the nature and amount of the service for each day for which compensation is claimed: *Provided,* That in no case shall the county com- `Proviso.` missioner receive any order for compensation from the county clerk until he has filed a certified statement from the Superintendent of Public Instruction that all reports required of the commissioner have been properly made and filed with said superintendent: *Provided further,* That no `Further proviso.` commissioner shall receive an order for compensation until he shall have filed with the county clerk a detailed statement under oath showing what schools have been visited by him during the preceding quarter and what amount of time was employed in each school, naming the township and school district. The necessary contingent expenses of `Of contingent expenses.` the commissioner for printing, postage, stationery, record books and rent of rooms for public examinations shall be audited and allowed by the board of supervisors of the county, but in no county shall the expenses so allowed `Limit of.`

exceed the sum of two hundred dollars per annum and no traveling fees shall be allowed to the commissioner or to any assistant visitor or school examiner.

Shall not act as agent, etc.

SEC. 11. No county commissioner shall act as agent for the sale of any school furniture, text-books, maps, charts or other school apparatus, nor be interested financially in any summer normal, or teachers' training class in the county for which he was elected.

Of vacancies.

SEC. 12. Whenever by death, resignation, removal from office or otherwise a vacancy shall occur in the office of the county commissioner of schools, the county clerk shall issue a call to the chairman of the township board of school inspectors of each township in the county, who shall meet at the office of the county clerk on a date to be named in said [notices] notice not more than ten days from the date of the notice, and appoint a suitable person to fill the vacancy for the unexpired portion of the term of office.

Certain schools exempted, etc.

SEC. 13. All schools which by special enactment may have a district board authorized to inspect and grant certificates to the teachers employed in the same, shall be exempt from the provisions of this act, as to the examina-

Of city schools.

tion and licensing of teachers. The officers of every school district which is or shall hereafter be organized in whole or in part in any incorporated city in this State where no special enactments shall exist in regard to the licensing of teachers shall have power to examine and license, or may require the county commissioner to examine and license teachers for such district and such license shall be valid in

Exempt from licensing of teachers, etc.

said district for the term of three years. All city schools having a superintendent employed by their respective boards of education shall be exempt from the provisions of this chapter as to the examination and licensing of teachers and

To make reports.

as to the supervision of the schools in such city, but all such schools shall, through their proper officers, make such reports as the Superintendent of Public Instruction may require.

Repealing clause.

SEC. 14. All acts or parts of acts conflicting with the provisions of this act are hereby repealed.

NOTE 1. The present secretary shall continue to act under the provisions of the old law until the fourth Tuesday of August.

NOTE 2. The members of the old board of examiners other than the secretary shall act with the school commissioner until the second Monday of October, when the term of the examiners under this act will begin.

[ACT No. 176.]

[Takes effect June 30, 1891.]

AN ACT for the organization of township school districts
in the Upper Peninsula.

SECTION 1. *The People of the State of Michigan enact,* Petition for
That whenever the qualified electors of any organized town- organization.
ship in the Upper Peninsula desire to become organized into
a single school district, they may petition the township
board to give notice that at the succeeding township meeting
the officers for such organized school district will be chosen,
and such other business transacted as shall be necessary
thereto. ˙Such petition shall be signed by a majority of the
qualified electors of the township and shall be filed in the
office of the township clerk at least fifteen days prior to the
annual township meeting. Upon the receipt and filing of Clerk to notify
said petition, the township clerk shall notify the members board, etc.
of the township board and the school [inspector] inspectors
of the township to attend a special meeting to be held not
more than five days thereafter, and at which meeting it shall
be the duty of such township board to compare the names
signed to the petition with the names appearing on the list
of registered voters qualified to vote at the preceding election,
and if it be found that a majority of the voters qualified
to vote at the preceding election have signed the petition
that the organized township of which they are resident be
organized as a single school district, they shall give notice
that at the then succeeding township meeting officers will
be chosen for such organized school district; and shall make
and file, both with the county clerk and the secretary* of
the board of school inspectors of the county in which such
township is located, a certified copy of the above mentioned petition together with their finding and doings thereon, and thereupon such township shall become a single school To be single
district which shall be subject to all the general laws of the districts, etc.
State, so far as the same may be applicable, and said district
shall have all the powers and privileges conferred upon
union school districts by the laws of this State, all the general provisions of which relating to common or primary
schools shall apply and be enforced in said district, except
such as shall be inconsistent with the provisions of this
act, and all schools organized in said district in pursuance
of this act, under the directions and regulations of said
board of education shall be public and free to all persons
actual residents within the limits thereof, between the ages
of five and twenty years, inclusive, and to such other persons as the board of education shall admit: *Provided,* That Proviso.
whenever the majority of electors in any surveyed township in such organized township shall petition the board
of education to establish a school or schools therein, the
said board of education are hereby authorized and directed

* School Commissioner.

within three months thereafter to organize such school or schools therein.

Officers of district.

SEC. 2. The officers of said district shall consist of two trustees, who, together with the clerk and school inspector of said township, shall constitute the board of education of said district. Said trustees shall be elected by ballot at the annual township meeting of the township, upon the same ticket and canvassed in the same manner as township

Proviso.

officers required by law to be elected by ballot: *Provided,* That at the annual election to be held in said township next subsequent to the filing of the petition as set forth in section one of this act there shall be elected two trustees for said district by the electors thereof, one of whom shall hold his office for the term of one year, and the other one for the term of two years, and until their successors shall be elected and qualified, and the time for which the person voted for is intended, shall be designated on the ballot, and at each election thereafter to be held one trustee shall be elected in said district, who shall hold his office for the term of two years, and until his successor shall be elected and qualified, said trustee to be designated on the ticket or ballot for "Member of board education."

Duty of township clerk, etc.

SEC. 3. Within five days after the annual election the township clerk shall notify, in writing, the persons elected trustees under this act of their election, and within five days thereafter said trustees so elected shall take and subscribe the oath of office prescribed by the constitution of this State, before any officer authorized to administer oaths, and file the same with the township clerk. The term of office of the [trustee] trustees of said district shall commence on the second Monday following the annual township election at which they are elected.

Organization of board, etc.

SEC. 4. The members of the board of education shall meet on the third Monday of April of each year, at the office of the township clerk, and organize. The school inspector of the township whose term of office will soonest expire shall be president of the board and shall be entitled to vote in all cases. In the absence of the president at any meeting a majority of the members present may choose one

Clerk.

of their own number president *pro tem.* The township clerk of said township shall be *ex officio* clerk of said board of education, and shall be entitled to vote thereon, and in case of the absence of said clerk the board may choose

Treasurer.

some suitable person to perform his duties. Said board shall on said third Monday of April in each year elect from their own number a treasurer, who shall hold his office for one year and until his successor is elected and qualified and may at any time fill a vacancy in the office of treasurer:

Proviso.

Provided, That the person appointed to fill a vacancy in the office of treasurer shall hold the office for the unexpired portion of the term only. The treasurer of said board shall within five days after his appointment as such treasurer, file with the clerk of said board the constitutional oath of office. He shall also, before entering upon the duties of his office, give a bond to said district in such sum and with such sureties as said board shall determine and approve, conditioned for the faithful performance of his duties under this act, and honestly accounting for all moneys coming into his hands belonging to said district. The treasurer of said board shall have the keeping of all school and library moneys, and shall not pay out the same without the authority of the board, upon warrants or orders drawn upon him and signed by the clerk and countersigned by the president. *To give bond.*

SEC. 5. Said board of education shall have power to fill vacancies that may occur in the office of trustee until the next annual election, and such trustee shall file with the clerk of said board his oath of office within five days after such appointment by the board. *Vacancies.*

SEC. 6. A majority of the members of said board shall constitute a quorum, and the regular meetings of said board shall be held on the third Monday of April, August and December in each year, and no notice of such meeting shall be required, and any two members of said board shall be sufficient to adjourn any meeting from time to time until a quorum is present. Special meetings of said board may be called at any time on the request of the president, or any two members thereof, in writing, delivered to the clerk; and the clerk upon receiving such request shall at once notify each member of said board, if within said district, of the time of holding such meeting, which shall be at least three days subsequent to the time of receiving such request by said clerk. All [the] meetings of said board shall be held at the township clerk's office, unless otherwise ordered by a resolution of the board; and all records and papers of said district shall be kept in the custody of said clerk and shall be open to the inspection of any taxpayer of said district. *Quorum, meetings, etc.*

SEC. 7. The said board shall be the board of school [inspection] inspectors for said district and shall, as such, report to the clerk of the county in which such township is located and shall have all the powers and perform all the duties now enjoyed and performed by boards of school inspectors, and the president of said board shall perform all the duties required by law of the chairman of the board of school inspectors, and the board of school inspectors for such township is hereby abolished except as its powers are vested in said board of education. *Board to report, etc.*

SEC. 8. The board of education of said district shall have power and authority to designate and purchase school house sites, erect buildings and furnish the same, employ legally qualified teachers, provide books for district library, make by-laws relative to taking the census of all children in said *Powers of board, etc.*

3

district between the ages of five and twenty years, and to make all necessary reports and transmit the same to the proper officers, as designated by law, so that the district may be entitled to its proportion of the primary school fund; and said board shall have authority to make all needful regulations and by-laws relative to visitation of schools; relative to the length of time schools shall be kept, which shall not be less than three months in each year; relative to the employment of teachers duly and legally qualified; relative to the regulations of schools and the books to be used therein, and generally to do all things needful and desirable for the maintenance, prosperity and success of the schools of said district, and the promotion of a thorough education

Treasurer to apply for moneys. of the children thereof. It shall be the duty of the treasurer of said board to apply for and receive from the township treasurer or other officer holding the same, all moneys appropriated for primary [schools] school and district library of said district.

Tax for school purposes. SEC. 9. At each annual township meeting held in said township, the qualified electors present shall determine the amount of money to be raised by tax for all school purposes for the ensuing year: **Proviso.** *Provided,* That in case the electors at any annual township meeting shall neglect or refuse to determine the amount to be raised as aforesaid, then the board of education shall determine the same at any regular meeting thereof, which amount the township clerk shall, within sixty days thereafter, certify to the supervisor of the township, who shall spread the same upon the regular tax roll of said township, and the same shall be levied, collected and returned in the same manner as other township taxes: **Idem.** *Provided,* That for purchasing school lots and for erecting school houses, no greater sum than three mills on the dollar of all the taxable valuation of the real and personal property in said township shall be levied in any one year.

Of assessment roll. SEC. 10. All taxes assessed within said township for school purposes shall be set forth in the assessment roll of said township, in a separate column, apart and distinct from all other township taxes.

Treasurer to report, etc. SEC. 11. The treasurer of the township shall at any time, at the written request of said board of education, report to said board the amount of school money in his hands, and shall, on the order of the president of said board of education, pay to the treasurer of said board all such money, taking his receipt therefor, and also a duplicate receipt which he shall file with the clerk of said board.

Board to make statement, etc. SEC. 12. The said board shall annually, prior to the first day of April in each year, make a detailed statement of the number of schools in said district, the number of teachers employed, and the number of pupils instructed therein during the preceding year, and the expenditures of said board for all purposes, and also the resources and liabilities of said district, which report or statement shall be entered at length in the record of said board and shall be publicly read by the president of said board, or in his absence by the clerk thereof, to the electors of said township at their annual meeting on the first Monday of April thereafter, at the hour of twelve o'clock, noon.

SEC. 13. All school property, both real and personal, within the limits of a township incorporated as aforesaid, shall, by force of this act, become the property of the public schools of such township, and all debts and liabilities of the primary school districts of said township, as they existed prior to its incorporation under the provisions of this act, shall become the debts and liabilities of said public schools of the township so incorporated. *Disposition of school property.*

SEC. 14. All money raised or being raised by tax, or accrued or accruing to the school districts of said township, as organized under the primary school laws of this State shall hereby become the money of the public school of the township and no tax heretofore ordered assessed or levied for school purposes in said township or other proceedings shall be invalidated or affected by means of this act. *Of moneys raised by tax.*

SEC. 15. The compensation of the members of the board of education shall be one dollar and fifty cents for each day's actual service rendered for said district, and the clerk and treasurer of said board shall receive such compensation for their services as the board may determine, not exceeding fifty dollars each per annum. *Compensation of board, etc.*

SEC. 16. When any township district shall be divided into two or more townships, the existing board of trustees shall continue to act for all the townships until the same have been organized and township boards of trustees duly elected and qualified therein. Immediately after such organization, the township boards of each of the townships shall meet in joint session and direct an appraisal of all the school property of the former township to be made. When such appraisal has been made, said township boards shall make an equitable division of the existing assets and liabilities of the school district of such former township, basing their apportionment upon the amount of taxable property in the township divided, as shown by the last assessment roll of such former township. When a township district shall be altered in its limits by annexing a portion of its territory to another township or townships, the township boards of each of the townships shall, immediately after such alteration, meet in joint session and make an equitable division of the assets and liabilities of the school district of the township from which the territory has been detached, basing their division upon the amount of taxable property, as the same shall appear upon the last assessment roll of such township. *When township is divided, etc.* *Alteration of township, etc.*

THE
GENERAL SCHOOL LAWS

OF

MICHIGAN:

WITH

APPENDIXES.

COMPILED AT THE OFFICE OF THE

ГRUCTION.

BY AUTHORITY.

LANSING:
DARIUS D. THORP, STATE PRINTER AND BINDER.
1889.

THE

GENERAL SCHOOL LAWS

OF

MICHIGAN:

WITH

APPENDIXES.

COMPILED AT THE OFFICE OF THE

SUPERINTENDENT OF PUBLIC INSTRUCTION.

1889.

BY AUTHORITY.

LANSING:
DARIUS D. THORP, STATE PRINTER AND BINDER.
1889.

THIS VOLUME IS STATE PROPERTY.

INTRODUCTORY.

This compilation of the General School Laws includes all constitutional and statutory provisions relating to education at present in force. The amendments passed at the legislative sessions of 1887 and 1889 have been incorporated in the text, necessitating some slight changes in the arrangement followed in the edition of 1885. Act No. 222, Public Acts of 1887, relating to truancy, and Act No. 147, Public Acts of 1889, providing for free text-books, are added as new chapters. With these additions, and a slight change in numbering the compiler's sections in the latter part of the text, the general plan of the edition of 1885 has been closely followed.

The opinions of Attorneys General that have from time to time been filed in the office of the Superintendent of Public Instruction are given in foot notes, with references to the section or sections containing the provisions of law covered by the decision. It is believed that these decisions will prove of much assistance in arriving at a proper construction of the law, and will aid school officers very materially in solving many of the perplexing questions that continually arise.

The digest of Supreme Court decisions embodied in Appendix A has been brought up to date and the index carefully revised.

JOSEPH ESTABROOK,
Superintendent of Public Instruction.

CONTENTS.

GENERAL

SCHOOL LAWS OF MICHIGAN.

CONSTITUTIONAL PROVISIONS.

ARTICLE VIII.

STATE OFFICERS.

SECTION 1. There shall be elected at each biennial election, a secretary of state, a superintendent of public instruction, a state treasurer, commissioner of the land office, an auditor general, and an attorney general, for the term of two years. They shall keep their offices at the seat of government, and shall perform such duties as may be prescribed by law.

SEC. 2. Their term of office shall commence on the first day of January, one thousand eight hundred and fifty-three, and of every second year thereafter.

SEC. 3. Whenever a vacancy shall occur in any of the State offices, the governor shall fill the same by appointment, by and with the advice and consent of the senate, if in session.

ARTICLE XIII.

EDUCATION.

SECTION 1. The superintendent of public instruction shall have the general supervision of public instruction, and his duties shall be prescribed by law.

SEC. 2. The proceeds from the sales of all lands that have been or hereafter may be granted by the United States to the State for educational purposes, and the proceeds of all lands or other property given by individuals, or appropriated by the State for like purposes, shall be and remain a perpetual fund, the interest and income of which, together with the rents of all such lands as may remain unsold, shall be inviolably appropriated and annually applied to the specific objects of the original gift, grant or appropriation.

Escheats.

SEC. 3. All lands, the titles to which shall fail from a defect of heirs, shall escheat to the State; and the interest on the clear proceeds from the sales thereof shall be appropriated exclusively to the support of primary schools.

Free schools.

SEC. 4. The legislature shall, within five years from the adoption of this constitution, provide for and establish a system of primary schools, whereby a school shall be kept without charge for tuition, at least three months in each year, in every school district in the State; and all instruction in said schools shall be conducted in the English language.

Instruction conducted in English language.

District schools.

SEC. 5. A school shall be maintained in each school district at least three months in each year. Any school district neglecting to maintain such school shall be deprived for the ensuing year of its proportion of the income of the primary school fund, and of all funds arising from taxes for the support of schools.

When deprived of public money.

Election of regents of the university.

SEC. 6. There shall be elected in the year eighteen hundred and sixty-three, at the time of the election of a justice of the supreme court, eight regents of the university, two of whom shall hold their office for two years, two for four years, two for six years, and two for eight years. They shall enter upon the duties of their office on the first of January next succeeding their election. At every regular election of a justice of the supreme court thereafter, there shall be elected two regents, whose term of office shall be eight years. When a vacancy shall occur in the office of regent, it shall be filled by appointment of the governor. The regents thus elected shall constitute the board of regents of the university of Michigan.[1]

Vacancy, how filled.

Regents a body corporate.

SEC. 7. The regents of the university, and their successors in office, shall continue to constitute the body corporate known by the name and title of "The regents of the university of Michigan."

President of the university.

SEC. 8. The regents of the university shall, at their first annual meeting, or as soon thereafter as may be, elect a president of the

[1] Amendment agreed to by the legislature of 1861, and approved by the people in 1862.

university, who shall be *ex officio* a member of their board, with the privilege of speaking, but not of voting. He shall preside at the meetings of the regents, and be the principal executive officer of the university. The board of regents shall have the general supervision of the university, and the direction and control of all expenditures from the university interest fund. University interest fund.

SEC. 9. There shall be elected at the general election in the year one thousand eight hundred and fifty-two, three members of a State board of education; one for two years, one for four years and one for six years; and at each succeeding biennial election there shall be elected one member of such board, who shall hold his office for six years. The superintendent of public instruction shall be *ex officio* a member and secretary of such board. The board shall have the general supervision of the State normal school, and their duties shall be prescribed by law. State board of education. Superintendent of public instruction a member. Care of normal school.

SEC. 10. Institutions for the benefit of those inhabitants who are deaf, dumb, blind or insane, shall always be fostered and supported. Asylums.

SEC. 11. The legislature shall encourage the promotion of intellectual, scientific and agricultural improvement; and shall, as soon as practicable, provide for the establishment of an agricultural school. The legislature may appropriate the twenty-two sections of salt spring lands now unappropriated, or the money arising from the sale of the same, where such lands have been already sold, and any land which may hereafter be granted or appropriated for such purpose, for the support and maintenance of such school, and may make the same a branch of the university, for instruction in agriculture and the natural sciences connected therewith, and place the same under the supervision of the regents of the university. Agricultural school.

SEC. 12. The legislature shall also provide for the establishment of at least one library in each township and city; and all fines assessed and collected in the several counties and townships for any breach of the penal laws, shall be exclusively applied to the support of such libraries, unless otherwise ordered by the township board of any township, or the board of education of any city: *Provided,* That in no case shall such fines be used for other than library or school purposes.[1] Libraries. Penal fines to be applied for libraries. Proviso.

---

[1] Amendment agreed to by the legislature of 1879, and approved by the people in 1881.

STATUTORY PROVISIONS.

Act No. 164, Laws of 1881, as amended by Session Laws of 1883, 1885, 1887 and 1889.

CHAPTER I.

THE SUPERINTENDENT OF PUBLIC INSTRUCTION.

Powers and duties of.

(§1.) SECTION 1. *The People of the State of Michigan enact,* That the superintendent of public instruction shall have general supervision of public instruction and of all State institutions, other than the university, that are essentially educational in their character, and it shall be his duty, among other things, to visit the university, the agricultural college, the institution for the deaf and dumb, the school for the blind, the reform school, the reform school for girls, and the public school for dependent and neglected children, and to meet with the governing boards

To make annual report.

of each of said institutions at least once in each year. He shall also prepare annually, and transmit to the governor, to be by him transmitted to the legislature at each biennial session thereof, a report containing:

Contents of.

First, A statement of the condition of the university and of each of the several State educational institutions, all incorporated institutions of learning, and the primary, graded, and high schools;

Second, Estimates and amounts of expenditures of all educational funds;

Third, Plans for the management of all educational funds, and for the better organization of the educational system, if, in his opinion, the same be required;

Fourth, The annual reports and accompanying documents, so far as he shall deem the same of sufficient public interest, of all State institutions of educational character;

Fifth, Abstracts of the annual reports of the school inspectors of the several townships and cities of the State;

Sixth, All such other matter relating to his office and the subject of education generally as he shall deem expedient to communicate.

Deputy superintendent.

(§2.) SEC. 2. He may appoint a deputy superintendent of public instruction and revoke such appointment in his discretion, and such deputy shall take the constitutional oath of office, which with his appointment, shall be filed with the secretary of state.

Duties of.

Said deputy may execute the duties of the office in case of a vacancy or the absence of the superintendent.

School laws to be compiled and published with forms, etc.

(§3.) SEC. 3. The superintendent of public instruction shall compile and cause to be printed all general laws relating to schools, together with all necessary forms, regulations, and instructions for conducting all proceedings under said laws, or relative to the organization and government of the schools, including rules and regulations for the management of township and district libraries, and shall transmit the same to the several officers intrusted with the care and managment of said schools.

(§4.) SEC. 4. He shall semi-annually, on receiving notice from the auditor general of the amounts thereof, and between the first and tenth days of May and November, apportion the primary school interest fund among the several townships and cities of the State, in proportion to the number of children in each between the ages of five and twenty years, as the same shall appear by the reports of the several boards of school inspectors made to him for the school year closing prior to the May apportionment, and shall prepare a statement of the amount in the aggregate payable to each county, and shall deliver the same to the auditor general, who shall thereupon draw his warrant upon the State treasurer in favor of the treasurer of each county for the amount payable to each county. He shall also send written notices to the clerks of the several counties of the amount in the aggregate to be disbursed in their respective counties, and the amount payable to the townships and cities therein respectively.* *[Apportionment of primary school fund, etc. See App. A., 154. Notice to county clerks of amounts disbursed.]*

(§5.) SEC. 5. Whenever the returns from any county, township, city, or district, upon which a statement of the amount to be disbursed or paid to any such county, township, city, or district shall be so far defective as to render it impracticable to ascertain the share of primary school interest fund which ought to be disbursed or paid to such county, township, city, or district, he shall ascertain by the best evidence in his power the facts upon which the ratio of such apportionment shall depend, and shall make the apportionment accordingly. *[Proceedings in case of defective returns.]*

(§6.) SEC. 6. Whenever any county, township, city, or district, through failure or error in making the proper report, shall fail to receive its share of the primary school interest fund, the superintendent of public instruction, upon satisfactory proof that said county, township, city, or district was justly entitled to the same, shall apportion such deficiency in his next apportionment; and whenever it shall appear to the satisfaction of said superintendent that any district has had three months' school, but failed to have the full time of school required by law, through no fault or negligence of the district or its officers, he may include such district in his apportionment of the primary school interest fund in his discretion. *[When deficiency may be apportioned the next year.]*

(§7.) SEC. 7. The superintendent of public instruction shall perform such other duties as are or shall be required of him by law, and at the expiration of his term of office deliver to his successor all property, books, documents, maps, records, reports, and all other papers belonging to his office, or which may have been received by him for the use of his office. *[Other duties of superintendent.]*

* As amended by Act No. 202, Session Laws of 1885.

CHAPTER II.

FORMATION, ALTERATION, MEETINGS, AND POWERS OF DISTRICTS.

Inspectors to
form districts.

(§8.) SECTION 1. The township board of school inspectors shall divide the township into such number of school districts as may from time to time be necessary, which districts they shall number,

May alter
boundaries of.

and they may regulate and alter the boundaries of the same as circumstances shall render proper, subject to the provisions here-

See App. A.,
¶ 48.

inafter made; but no district shall contain more than nine sections of land, and each district shall be composed of contiguous territory, and be in as compact a form as may be.

Township clerk
to deliver notice
of formation to
inhabitant.

(§9.) SEC. 2. Whenever the board of school inspectors of any township shall form a school district therein, it shall be the duty of the clerk of such board to deliver to a taxable inhabitant of

See App. B.,
forms 1, 2, 3.

such district a notice in writing of the formation of such district, describing its boundaries, and specifying the time and place of the first meeting, which notice, with the fact of such delivery,

Inhabitant to
serve notice of
first meeting.

shall be entered upon record by the clerk. The said notice shall also direct such inhabitant to notify every qualified voter of such district, either personally or by leaving a written notice at his place of residence, of the time and place of said meeting, at least

See ¶ 139.

five days before the time appointed therefor; and it shall be the duty of such inhabitant to notify the qualified voters of said district accordingly, and said inhabitant, when he shall have

Return of
notice.
Notice and
return to be
recorded.

notified the qualified voters as required in such notice, shall indorse thereon a return, showing such notification with the date or dates thereof, and deliver such notice and return to the chairman of the meeting, to be by him delivered to the director chosen at such meeting, and by said director recorded at length as a part of the records of such district.

Proceedings in
case of failure
to organize
district.

(§10.) SEC. 3. In case the inhabitants of any district shall fail to organize the same in pursuance of such notice as aforesaid, the said clerk shall give a new notice in the manner hereinbefore provided, and the same proceedings shall be had thereon as if no previous notice had been delivered.

Formation of
fractional
districts.

(§11.) SEC. 4. Whenever it shall be necessary or convenient to form a district from two or more adjoining townships, the inspectors, or a majority of them, of each of such adjoining townships, may form such district, to be designated as a fractional district, and direct which township clerk shall make and deliver the notice of the formation of the same to a taxable inhabitant thereof, and may regulate and alter such district as circumstances may render necessary in the same manner that other districts are

To whom
director of such
district shall
report.

altered. The annual reports of the director of such district shall be made to the inspectors of the township in which the school.

(§8.) In Clement vs. Everest, 29 Mich., page 19, the Supreme Court decided that the legality of the action of the officers in organizing a school district cannot be enquired into collaterally; that it is none of the business of the township treasurer whether the district was or was not properly organized and that he must go on in the performance of his duties with respect thereto until such organization has been declared illegal on a proceeding instituted for that purpose.—*Kirchner, Atty. Gen., Aug. 20, 1878.*

house may be situated, and the inspectors of such township shall number said district.

(§12.) SEC. 5. Every such school district shall be deemed duly organized when any two of the officers elected at the first meeting shall have filed their acceptances in writing with the director, and the same shall have been recorded in the minutes of such first meeting. Every school district shall, in all cases, be presumed to have been legally organized when it shall have exercised the franchises and privileges of a district for the term of two year; and such school district and its officers shall be entitled to all the rights, privileges, and immunities, and be subject to all the duties and liabilities conferred upon school districts by law. *When district deemed organized.* *Presumption of legal organization.* *See App. A., ¶¶ 25, 29, 39, 47.*

(§13.) SEC. 6. The record of the first meeting made by the director shall be *prima facie* evidence of the facts therein set forth, and of the legality of all proceedings in the organization of the district prior to the first district meeting; but nothing in this section contained shall be so construed as to impair the effect of the record kept by the school inspectors, as evidence. *Director's record of first meeting to be evidence.*

CORPORATE POWERS OF DISTRICTS.

(§14.) SEC. 7. Every school district organized in pursuance of this chapter, or which has been organized and continued under any previous law of the State or territory of Michigan, shall be a body corporate, and shall possess the usual powers of a corporatoin for public purposes, by the name and style of "School District Number —— (such number as shall be designated in the formation thereof by the inspectors), of ——" (the name of the township or townships in which the district is situated), and in that name shall be capable of suing and being sued, of contracting and being contracted with, and of holding such real and personal estate as is authorized to be purchased by the provisions of law, and of selling the same. *School districts to be bodies corporate.* *Name and style.* *Powers of.*

ALTERATION OF DISTRICTS.

(§15.) SEC. 8. Whenever the board of school inspectors shall contemplate an alteration of the boundaries of a district, the township clerk (and for meetings of boards to act in relation to fractional districts, clerks of the several townships interested) shall give at least ten days' notice of the time and place of the meeting of the inspectors, and the alterations proposed, by posting such notice in three public places in the township or townships, one of which notices shall be in each of the districts that may be affected by such alteration. Whenever the board of school inspectors of more than one township meet, they shall elect one of their number chairman, and another clerk thereof.[b] *Meetings of inspectors to alter districts.* *Notice of.* *See App. B., form 16.* *See App. A., ¶¶ 1, 36, 38, 46.*

(§16.) SEC. 9. The inspectors may, in their discretion, detach the property of any person or persons from one district and attach it to another; except that no land which has been taxed *Powers of inspectors to alter districts.*

---

[b] As amended by Act No. 82, Session Laws of 1883.

See App. A., ¶¶ 2, 3, 37, 41, 42, 43, 45, 98.

When consent of tax-payers to be obtained.

See § 110.

for building a school-house shall be set off into another school district for the period of three years thereafter, except by the consent of the owner thereof; and no district shall be divided into two or more districts without the consent of a majority of the resident tax-payers of said district, and no two or more districts be consolidated without the consent of a majority of the resident tax-payers of each district.

Persons out of district may be attached thereto in certain cases.

(§17.) SEC. 10. The inspectors may attach to a school district any person residing in a township, and not in any organized district, at his request; and for all district purposes except raising a tax for building a school-house, such person shall be considered as residing in such district; but when set off to a new district, no sum shall be raised for such person as his proportion to the district property.

Township clerk to give notice of alteration in districts.

See App. B., form 4.

(§18.) SEC. 11. In all cases where an alteration of the boundaries of a school district shall be made, the township clerk shall, within ten days, deliver to the director of each district affected by the alteration a notice in writing, setting forth the action of the inspectors and defining the alterations that have been made.

DIVISION OF PROPERTY.

When district is divided property to be apportioned.

See App. A., ¶¶ 3, 4, 40, 98, 105.

When school-house or site is not needed, may be sold.

See App. A., ¶ 44.

Proceeds of sale to be apportioned.

(§ 19.) SEC. 12. When a new district is formed in whole or in part, from one or more districts possessed of a school-house, or entitled to other property, the inspectors, at the time of forming such new district, or as soon thereafter as may be, shall ascertain and determine the amount justly due to such new district from any district out of which it may have been in whole or in part formed, as the proportion of such new district, of the value of the school-house and other property belonging to the former district, at the time of such division; and whenever by the division of any district, the school-house or site thereof shall no longer be conveniently located for school purposes, and shall not be desired for use by the new district in which it may be situated, the school inspectors of the township in which such school-house and site shall be located, may advertise and sell the same, and apportion the proceeds of such sale, and also any moneys belonging to the district thus divided, among the several districts erected in whole or in part from the divided district.

How proportion to be ascertained.

Proviso.

(§ 20.) SEC. 13. Such proportion shall be ascertained and determined according to the value of the taxable property of the respective parts of such former district at the time of the division, by the best evidence in the power of the inspectors; and such amount of any debt due from the former district, which would have been a charge upon the new, had it remained in the former district, shall be deducted from such proportion : *Provided*, That no real estate thus set off, and which shall not have been taxed for the purchase or building of such school-house,

(§ 19.) Upon investigation we are of the opinion that the school inspectors of the township have full and absolute control over the advertisement, sale and apportionment of the proceeds among the several districts, erected in whole or in part therefrom.—*VanRiper, Attorney General, July 24, 1882.*

shall be entitled to any portion thereof, nor be taken into account in such division of district property.

DISTRICT MEETINGS.

(§ 21.) SEC. 14. The annual meeting of each school district shall be held on the first Monday of September in each year, and the school year shall commence on that day: *Provided,* That any school district that shall so determine at an annual meeting, or at a special meeting duly called for that purpose, may hold its annual meeting on the second Monday of July in each year, or in the same manner may thereafter change the time of its annual meeting to the first Monday in September in each year, and the trustees and officers of the district shall date their terms of office from the date so chosen and until their successors are elected and qualified: *Provided further,* That such action in either case shall not change the time of the commencement of the school year or the taking of the annual school census.[c] *Annual meeting. School year. Date of annual meeting may be changed. Proviso.*

(§ 22.) SEC. 15. Special meetings may be called by the district board; and it shall be the duty of said board, or any one of them, to call such meetings on the written request of not less than five legal voters of the district, by giving the notice required in the next succeeding section; but no special meeting shall be called unless the business to be transacted may lawfully come before such meeting, and no business shall be transacted at a special meeting unless the same be stated in the notice of said meeting. *Special meetings. See App. D., form 8. When may not be called. Business of to be stated in notice.*

(§23.) SEC. 16. All notices of annual or special district meetings, after the first meeting has been held as aforesaid, shall specify the day, and hour and place of meeting, and shall be given at least six days previous to such meeting, by posting up copies thereof in three of the most public places in the district, one copy of which for each meeting shall be posted at the outer door of the district schoolhouse, if there be one; and in case of any special meeting called for the purpose of establishing or changing the site of a schoolhouse, such notice shall be given at least ten days previous thereto: *Provided,* That when any of the district board shall receive a request to call a special meeting, as provided in the preceding section, he shall forthwith give notice, as above provided, of said meeting, which shall be called in not less than six nor more than twelve days from the time the said officer shall receive the notice aforesaid. No annual meeting shall be deemed illegal for want of due notice, unless it shall appear that the omission to give such notice was willful and fraudulent. *Notice of meetings. See App. B., forms 7, 9. Duty of district officer to give notice. When annual meeting not illegal for want of notice.*

(§24.) SEC. 17. Every person of the age of twenty-one years, who has property liable to assessment for school taxes in any school district, and who has resided therein three months next preceding any school meeting held in said district, or who has *Who are qualified voters at district meetings.*

[c] As amended by Act No. 22, Session Laws 1885.

(§24.). A person who has no property within the school district liable to assessment for school taxes has no right to vote when the raising of money by tax is in question. —*Kirchner, Attorney General, Sept. 20, 1877.*

resided three months next preceding such meeting on any territory belonging to such district at the time of holding said meeting, shall be a qualified voter in said meeting upon all questions, and all other persons who are twenty-one years of age, and are the parents or legal guardians of any children included in the school census of the district, and who have for three months as aforesaid, been residents of said district or upon any territory belonging thereto at the time of holding any school meeting, shall be entitled to vote on all questions arising in said district which do not directly involve the raising of money by tax.

Challenging voters. (§25.) SEC. 18. If any person offering to vote at a school district meeting shall be challenged as unqualified by any legal voter in such district, the chairman presiding at such meeting shall declare to the person challenged the qualifications of a voter; and if such person shall state that he is qualified, and the challenge shall not be withdrawn, the said chairman shall tender to him an oath, in **Oaths to be tendered challenged voters.** substance as follows: "You do swear (or affirm) that you are twenty-one years of age, that you have been for the last three months an actual resident of this school district, or residing upon territory now attached to this school district, and that you are liable to pay a school district tax therein;" and every person taking such oath shall be permitted to vote on all questions proposed at such meeting. Or he may take the following oath, to wit: "You do swear (or affirm) that you have been for the past three months an actual resident of this school district, or residing upon territory now attached to this school district, and that you are the parent or legal guardian of one or more children now included in the school census of this district;" and he may vote upon all questions which do not directly involve the raising of money by tax. **False oath deemed perjury.** If any person so challenged shall refuse to take such oath, his vote shall be rejected; and any person who shall willfully take a false oath, or make a false affirmation, under the provisions of this section, shall be deemed guilty of perjury. When any question is taken in any other manner than by ballot, a challenge shall be deemed immediately after the vote has been taken to be made when offering to vote, and treated in the same manner.

Disorderly persons at district meetings to be taken into custody. (§26.) SEC. 19. If at any district meeting any person shall conduct himself in a disorderly manner, and, after notice from the moderator or person presiding, shall persist therein, the moderator or person presiding may order him to withdraw from the meeting, and on his refusal, may order any constable, or other person or persons, to take him into custody until the meeting **Penalty for disturbing meeting.** shall be adjourned; and any person who shall refuse to withdraw from such meeting on being so ordered as herein provided, and also any person who shall willfully disturb such meeting by rude and indecent behavior, or by profane or indecent discourse, or in any other way make such disturbance, shall, on conviction thereof, be punished by a fine not less than two nor more than fifty dollars, or by imprisonment in the county jail not exceeding **Who shall have jurisdiction in trial.** thirty days; and any justice of the peace, recorder, or police justice of the township, ward, or city where such offense shall be committed, shall have jurisdiction to try and determine the same.

(§27.) SEC. 20. The qualified voters in any school district when lawfully assembled at the first and at each annual meeting, or at an adjournment thereof, or at any special meeting lawfully called, except as hereinafter provided, shall have power: *Powers of voters at district meetings.*

First, At the first meeting and at any meeting after the organization of the district, in the absence of the moderator, to appoint a chairman for the time being, and in the absence of the director to appoint some person to act in his stead, who shall keep a minute of the proceedings of such meeting and certify the same to the director, to be by him entered in the records of the district; *To appoint temporary officers.*

Second, To adjourn from time to time as occasion may require; *May adjourn.*

Third, To elect district officers as hereinafter provided; *To elect officers. See §§ 28, 107.*

Fourth, To designate, as hereinafter provided, a site or such number of sites as may be desired for school-houses, and to change the same when necessary; *To designate sites for school-houses. See § 89.*

Fifth, To direct the purchasing or leasing of a site or sites, lawfully determined upon; the building, hiring, or purchasing of a school-house or houses, or the enlarging of a site or sites previously established; *To direct purchase, etc., of site, and building school-houses.*

Sixth, To vote such tax as the meeting shall deem sufficient, to purchase or lease a site or sites, or to build, hire or purchase a school-house or houses; but the amount of taxes to be raised in any district for the purpose of purchasing or building a school-house or houses in the same year that any bonded indebtedness is incurred, shall not exceed in districts containing less than ten children between the ages of five and twenty years, two hundred and fifty dollars; in districts having between ten and thirty children of like age, it shall not exceed five hundred dollars; and in districts having between thirty and fifty children of like age, it shall not exceed one thousand dollars. No legal subdivisions [subdivision] of land shall be taxed for building a school-house unless some portion thereof shall be within two and one-half miles of said school-house site. *To vote tax for building, etc.* *Limit of tax.* *See § 78.* *When land not taxable.*

Seventh, To impose such tax as shall be necessary to keep their school-house or houses in repair, and to provide the necessary appendages and school apparatus, and in districts having district libraries, for the support of the same, and to pay and discharge any debts or liabilities of the district lawfully incurred, and also to pay for the services of any district officer. The tax herein authorized to be voted shall not exceed one-half the amount which the district is authorized to raise for building school-houses. *To vote tax for certain purposes. See App. A., ¶¶ 97, 101.* *Limit of tax.*

(§27, par. fifth). [In relation to power of school district to acquire land for enlargement of site]. It seems the owner of the land refuses to sell, and the question arises as to the proper method of obtaining such land for the enlargement of the site. I find nothing whatever in the act, save that in Chapter VIII, section 2 *et. seq.*, and this says nothing whatever about the enlargement of sites; yet land for enlargement is, I think, within the meaning of the act, and as there are no other provisions of law by which to obtain an enlarged site, where the owner refuses to sell, it is advisable to proceed thereunder, and if it does not cover cases of enlargement of site, let the courts so decide and the law must then be amended.—*Van Riper, Atty. Gen., March 21, 1889.*

To direct sale of certain property.

Eighth, To authorize and direct the sale of any school-house, site, building or other property belonging to the district, when the same shall no longer be needed for the use of the district;

Direct in regard to suits.

Ninth, To give such directions and make such provisions as they shall deem necessary in relation to the prosecution or defense of any suit or proceeding in which the district may be a party, or interested;

May appoint building committee.

Tenth, To appoint, as in their discretion it may be necessary, a building committee to perform such duties in supervising the work of building a school-house as they by vote may direct;

At annual meeting to determine limit of school.

Eleventh, At the first and the annual meetings only, to determine the length of time a school shall be taught in their district during the ensuing year, which shall not be less than nine months in districts having eight hundred children over five and

Forfeiture of public moneys.

under twenty years of age, and not less than five months in districts having from thirty to eight hundred children of like ages, nor less than three months in all other districts, on pain of forfeiture of their share of the one-mill tax and primary school interest fund; but in case such matters shall not be determined at the first or annual meetings, the district board shall determine

When district board to determine length of school.

the same; and in case the district fails to vote for at least the minimum length required herein, the district board shall make provisions for said minimum length of school;

May appropriate surplus mill-tax to certain purposes.

Twelfth, To appropriate any surplus moneys arising from the one-mill tax, after having maintained a school in the district at least eight months in the school year, for the purpose of purchasing and enlarging school sites, or for building or repairing school-houses, or for purchasing books for library, globes, maps, and other school apparatus, or for any incidental expenses of the school.

CHAPTER III.

DISTRICT BOARD AND OFFICERS.

Election of district officers.

See App. A., ¶¶ 151, 152.

See §§ 140, 147.

See App. A., ¶ 49.

Term of office.

(§28.) SECTION 1. At the first meeting in each school district there shall be elected by ballot a moderator for the term of three years, a director for two years, and an assessor for one year; and on the expiration of their respective terms of office, and regularly thereafter at the annual meetings, their several successors shall be elected in like manner for a term of three years each. The time intervening between the first meeting in any school district and the first annual meeting thereafter shall be reckoned as one year.

(§27, paragraph eight.)—All sales thus made shall be in the corporate name of the school district, as provided in section 7, chapter 2, of said act 164, while the deed or deeds of the conveyance of lands sold as above provided, shall be executed by the district board in their official capacity, but in the name of such district.—*VanRiper, Atty. Gen., July 24, 1883.*

(§28.) School district officers cannot be elected by a bare plurality vote. In electing officers the school district acts in its corporate capacity, and no corporate action can be had without the concurrence of the majority.—*Kirchner, Atty. Gen., July 18, 1877.*

(§29.) SEC. 2. A school district office shall become vacant upon the occurrence of any of the following events: When district offices shall become vacant.

First, The death of the incumbent;

Second, His resignation;

Third, His removal from office;

Fourth, His removal from the district;

Fifth, His conviction of any infamous crime;

Sixth, His election or appointment being declared void by a competent tribunal;

Seventh, His neglect to file his acceptance of office, or to give or renew any official bond, according to law.

(§30.) SEC. 3. In case any one of the district offices becomes vacant, the two remaining officers shall immediately fill such vacancy; or in case two of the offices become vacant, the remaining officer shall immediately call a special meeting of the district to fill such vacancies; in case any vacancy is not filled as herein provided within twenty days after it shall have occurred, or in case all the offices in a district shall become vacant, the board of school inspectors of the township to which the annual reports of such district are made shall fill such vacancies. Any person elected or appointed to fill a vacancy in a district office shall hold such office until the the next succeeding annual meeting, at which time the voters of the district shall fill such office for the unexpired portion of the term. Vacancies in office, how filled.
See App. B, forms 14, 15.
Term of office of appointed officer.

(§31.) SEC. 4. Any qualified voter in a school district who has property liable to assessment for school taxes shall be eligible to election or appointment to office in such school district, unless such person be an alien. Who are eligible to hold office.

(§32.) SEC. 5. Within ten days after their election or appointment, the several officers of each school district shall file with the director written acceptances of the offices to which they have been respectively elected or appointed, and such acceptances shall be entered in the records of the district by said director. Acceptances of offices to be filed.
See App. B., form 5.

(§33.) SEC. 6. The moderator, director, and assessor shall constitute the district board. Meetings of the board may be called by any member thereof by serving on the other members a written notice of the time and place of such meeting at least twenty-four hours before such meeting is to take place; and no act authorized to be done by the district board shall be valid unless voted at a meeting of the board. A majority of the members of the board at a meeting thereof shall be necessary for the transaction of business. District board, when meetings of, may be called.
Necessity of meeting to valid action by board.
Quorum of board.

(§29.) The temporary absence of the assessor does not create a vacancy in the office. If his family continues to reside in the district, and he has not actually removed, he retains his residence and with it his office. A removal is necessary, and a temporary absence, his family remaining, is not a removal, and there is no vacancy.—*Van Riper, Atty. Gen., Feb. 8, 1882.*

(§33.) The district board should act together. It is not necessary for valid official action that all the members should be consulted, but opportunity must be given to all the members to express their opinion and to vote upon the questions submitted to them.—*Kirchner, Atty. Gen., Dec. 4, 1877.*

(§33.) Whenever a power is vested in a board for a public purpose, it requires a quorum to act and a majority of that quorum to determine a matter before it.—*Kirchner, Atty. Gen., Apr. 7, 1879.*

(§34.) SEC. 7. The said district board shall purchase a record book and such other books, blanks, and stationery as may be necessary to keep a record of the proceedings of the district meetings and of meetings of the board, the accounts of the assessor, and for doing the business of the district in an orderly manner.

(§35.) SEC. 8. The district board shall purchase or lease, in the corporate name of the district, such sites for school-houses as shall have been lawfully designated, and shall build, hire, or purchase such school-houses as may be necessary out of the fund provided for that purpose, and make sale of any site or other property of the district when lawfully directed by the qualified voters; but no district in any case shall build a stone or brick school-house upon any site without having first obtained a title in fee to the same, or a lease for ninety-nine years; nor shall any district build a frame school-house on any site for which they have not a title in fee or a lease for fifty years, without securing the privilege of removing the said school-house when lawfully directed so to do by the qualified voters of the district at any annual or special meeting when lawfully convened.

(§36.) SEC. 9. It shall be the duty of the district board to estimate the amount necessary to be raised, in addition to other school funds, for the entire support of such schools, including teachers' wages, fuel, and other incidental expenses, and for deficiencies of the previous year for such purposes. But in districts having less than thirty scholars, such estimate, including the district's share of the primary school interest fund and one-mill tax, shall not exceed the sum of fifty dollars a month for the period during which school is held in such district; and when such amount has been estimated and voted by the district board, it shall be reported for assessment and collection, the same

as other district taxes. When a tax has been estimated and voted by the district board under the provisions of this section, and is needed before it can be collected, the district board may borrow to an amount not exceeding the amount of said tax.

(§37.) SEC. 10. The district board shall, between the first and third Mondays in September in each year, make out and deliver to the township clerk of each township in which any part of the district is situated, a report in writing under their hands of all taxes voted by the district during the preceding year, and of all taxes which said board is authorized to impose, to be levied on the taxable property of the district.

(§38.) SEC. 11. The district board shall apply and pay over all school moneys belonging to the district, in accordance with the provisions of law regulating the same, and no money raised by district tax shall be used for any other purpose than that for which it was raised, without a consenting vote of two-thirds of

---

(§35)—The record of a lease for a term of years is not essential to its validity, though leases for a longer term than three years should be recorded in order to render them effectual against subsequent purchasers in good faith and for a valuable consideration. The non payment of rent does not *ipso facto* terminate the lease.—*Kirchner, Atty. Gen., Sep. 26, 1877.*

the tax-paying voters of the district; and no moneys received from the primary school interest fund, nor from the one-mill tax except as provided by law shall be appropriated to any other use than the payment of teachers' wages, and no part thereof shall be paid to any teacher who shall not have received a certificate of qualification from proper legal authority before the commencement of his school. No school district shall apply any of the moneys received by it from the primary school interest fund, or from any and all other sources, for the support and maintenance of any school of a sectarian character, whether the same be under the control of any religious society, or made sectarian by the school district board. Sectarian schools barred from public moneys.

(§39.) SEC. 12. Said board shall present to the district, at each annual meeting, a report in writing, containing an accurate statement of all moneys of the district received by them, or any of them, during the preceding year, and of the disbursements made by them, with the items of such receipts and disbursements. Such report shall also contain a statement of all taxes assessed upon the taxable property of the district during the preceding year, the purposes for which such taxes were assessed, and the amount assessed for each particular purpose, and said report shall be entered by the director in the records of the district. Board to make annual report. Contents of.

(§40.) SEC. 13. The district board shall hire and contract with such duly qualified teachers as may be required; and all contracts shall be in writing and signed by a majority of the board on behalf of the district. Said contracts shall specify the wages agreed upon and shall require the teacher to keep a correct list of the pupils, and the age of each, attending the school, and the number of days each pupil is present, and to furnish the director with a correct copy of the same at the close of the school. Said contract shall be filed with the director, and a duplicate copy of the contract shall be furnished to the teacher. No contract with any person not holding a legal certificate of qualification then authorizing such person to teach shall be valid, and all such contracts shall terminate, if the certificate shall expire by limitation and shall not immediately be renewed, or if it shall be suspended or revoked by proper legal authority. A school month within the meaning of the school laws shall consist of four weeks of five days in each week, unless otherwise specified in the teacher's contract. Board to hire teachers. See App. B, forms 26, 27. Contracts. School register to be kept. See § 147. Contracts to be filed. Teacher must have legal certificate. See App. A., ¶¶ 79, 86, 90, 91, 92, 93, 94. School month defined.

(§41.) SEC. 14. The district board shall have the care and custody of the school-house and other property of the district, except so far as the same shall by vote of the district be specially confided to the custody of the director, including all books purchased for the use of indigent pupils, and shall open the school-house for public meetings unless by a vote at a district meeting it shall be determined otherwise: *Provided,* That said board may exclude such public meetings during the five school days of each Care and use of school house. Board may exclude public meetings at certain times.

(§33.) I am inclined to think that no money raised by district taxes can be used for any other purpose than that for which it was raised unless by vote of two-thirds of the tax paying voters of the district. I think this section must be strictly and literally observed.—*Kirchner, Atty. Gen., Sept. 26, 1877.*

week of any and all school terms, or such parts thereof as in their discretion they may deem for the best interest of the schools.

Board to specify studies and prescribe text-books.

(§42.) SEC. 15. The district board shall specify the studies to be pursued in the schools of the district [districts], and in addition to the branches in which instruction is now required by law to be given in the public schools of the State, instruction shall be given in physiology and hygiene with a special reference to the nature of alcohol and narcotics and their effects upon the human system. Such instruction shall be given by the aid of text-books in the case of pupils who are able to read and as thoroughly as in other studies pursued in the same school. The text-books to be used for such instruction shall give at least one-fourth of their space to the consideration of the nature and effects of alcoholic drinks and narcotics, and the books used in the highest grade of graded schools shall contain at least twenty pages of matter relating to this subject. Text-books used in giving the foregoing instruction shall first be approved by the State Board of Education. Each school board making a selection of text-books under the provisions of this act shall make a record thereof in their proceedings and text-books once adopted under the provisions of this act shall not be changed within five years except by the consent of a majority of the qualified voters of the district present at an annual meeting or at a special meeting called for that purpose. The district board shall require each teacher in the public schools of such district, before placing the school register in the hands of the directors [director] as provided in section thirteen of this act, to certify therein whether or not instruction has been given in the school or grade presided over by such teacher, as required by this act, and it shall be the duty of the director of the district to file with the township clerk a certified copy of such certificate. Any school board neglecting or refusing to comply with any of the provisions of this act, shall be subject to fine or forfeiture the same as for neglect of any other duty pertaining to their office. This act shall apply to all schools in the State, including schools in cities or villages, whether incorporated under special charter or under the general laws.[d]

Instruction in physiology and hygiene, etc., required.

Text-books in physiology, etc., to be approved by State board of education.

Purchase of books for poor children.

(§ 43.) SEC. 16. The district board may purchase at the expense of the district, such text-books as may be necessary for the use of children when parents are not able to furnish the same, and they shall include the amount of such purchase in the report to the township clerk or clerks, to be levied in like manner as other district taxes.

Board to establish rules for school.

See App. A., ¶ 64.

May suspend or expel disorderly pupils.

(§ 44.) SEC. 17. The district board shall have the general care of the school, and shall make and enforce suitable rules and regulations for its government and management, and for the preservation of the property of the district. Said board may authorize or order the suspension or expulsion from the school, whenever in its judgment the interests of the school demand it, of any

---

[d] As amended by act No. 93, public acts of 1883, and act No. 165, public acts of 1887.

pupil guilty of gross misdemeanor or persistent disobedience. Any person who shall disturb any school by rude and indecent behavior, or by profane or indecent discourse, or in any other way make such disturbance, shall, on conviction thereof, be punished by a fine not less than two nor more than fifty dollars, or by imprisonment in the county jail not exceeding thirty days. *Penalty for disturbing school.*

(§ 45.) Sec. 18. All persons residents of any school district, and five years of age, shall have an equal right to attend any school therein; and no separate school or department shall be kept for any persons on account of race or color: *Provided,* That this shall not be construed to prevent the grading of schools according to the intellectual progress of the pupil, to be taught in separate places as may be deemed expedient. *Who can attend school.* *No separate school on account of race, etc.* *See App. A., ¶ 113.* *Grading not prevented.*

(§ 46.) Sec. 19. The district board may admit to the district school non-resident pupils, and may determine the rates of tuition of such pupils, and collect the same. *Non-resident pupils.* *See App. A., ¶ 112.*

MODERATOR.

(§47.) Sec. 20. It shall be the duty of the moderator of each school district: *Moderator.*

First, To preside, when present, at all meetings of the district and of the board ; *To preside.*

Second, To countersign all orders legally drawn by the director upon the assessor for moneys to be disbursed by the district, and all warrants of the director upon the township treasurer for moneys raised for district purposes, or apportioned to the district by the township clerk ; *To countersign warrants and orders.* *See App. A., ¶¶ 55, 57.*

Third, To cause an action to be prosecuted in the name of the district on the assessor's bond, in case of any breach of any condition thereof; *To bring suit on assessor's bond.*

Fourth, To perform such other duties as are or shall be by law required of the moderator. *Other duties.*

DIRECTOR.

(§48.) Sec. 21. It shall be the duty of the director of each school district: *Director.*

First, To act as clerk, when present, at all meetings of the district and of the board ; *To be clerk.*

(§ 44.) It is not competent for the district board to assume the expense incurred in the legal defense of a teacher prosecuted for an assault alleged to have been made in the punishment of a pupil.—*Kirchner, Attorney General, Dec. 4, 1877.*

(§45.) The domicile of any person is the place which he has chosen for his permanent residence. Sometimes the law makes a distinction between "residence" and "domicile." Residence, contra distinguished from domicile, is the locality in which a person may reside for the time being. But in the case under consideration the term residence is used in the sense of domicile. I have no doubt that a person who makes Flint his or her home for no other purpose than to enjoy school privileges and with the intention of removing to his or her former home after the closing of the school is "not actually a resident of said district." A minor having parents living partakes of the domicile of his or her parents.—*Kirchner, Attorney General, Jan. 25, 1879.*

(§47.) The moderator should examine every order before countersigning it, and if it is drawn for an improper purpose, and with intent to defraud the district or to divert the fund from its proper channel, he should refuse to countersign such order, and the courts will sustain him in such action.—*VanRiper, Attorney General, Feb. 8, 1882.*

3

To keep and record minutes.	*Second,* To record the proceedings of all district meetings, and the minutes of all meetings, orders, resolutions, and other proceedings of the board, in proper record books;
To give notices of meetings. See App. B., forms 7, 9.	*Third,* To give the prescribed notice of the annual district meeting, and of all such special meetings as he shall be required to give notice of in accordance with the provisions of law;
To draw and sign warrants and orders. See App. A., ¶¶ 50, 66.	*Fourth,* To draw and sign warrants upon the township treasurer for all moneys raised for district purposes, or apportioned to the district by the township clerk, payable to the assessor of the district, and orders upon the assessor for all moneys to be disbursed by the district, and present them to the moderator, to
See App. B., forms 10, 11.	be countersigned by that officer. Each order shall specify the object for which, and the fund upon which, it is drawn;
To draw and sign contracts. See App. B., form 26.	*Fifth,* To draw and sign all contracts with teachers, when directed by the district board, and present them to the other members of the board for further signature;
To provide appendages and keep school-house in repair. Proviso. See App. A., ¶¶ 99, 101.	*Sixth,* To provide the necessary appendages for the school-house, and keep the same in good condition and repair during the time school shall be taught therein: *Provided,* That nothing herein contained shall be construed to authorize the director to purchase charts or any apparatus to be used in the school-room without a vote of the district authorizing the same;
To keep account.	*Seventh,* To keep an accurate account of all expenses incurred by him as director, and such account shall be audited by the moderator and assessor, and on their written order shall be paid out of any money provided for the purpose;
To present estimate of expenses to annual meeting.	*Eighth,* To present at each annual meeting an estimate of the expenses necessary to be incurred during the ensuing year by the director as provided by law, and for payment of the services of any district officer;
To preserve records and other documents.	*Ninth,* To preserve and file copies of all reports made to the school inspectors, and safely preserve and keep all books, papers, and other documents belonging to the office of director, or to the district when not otherwise provided for, and to deliver the same to his successor in office;
Other duties.	*Tenth,* To perform such other duties as are or shall be required of the director by law or the district board.
To take school census.	(§49.) SEC. 22. It shall be the duty of the director, or such other person as the district board may appoint, within ten days next previous to the first Monday in September in each year, to take the census of the district, and make a list in writing of the names and ages of all the children betwen the ages of five and
List to be sworn to.	twenty years residing therein, and a copy of said list shall be

(§48, paragraph six.) I think the director has power to provide new patent seats, if in his judgment such acquisition is "necessary." It is a general principle of law that whenever a power may be exercised by any person in certain emergencies, in the absence of any provision to the contrary, the person who is to execute the power must decide whether the emergency is sufficient for him to act. The director must decide what is necessary and he is responsible for any abuse of power. The word "necessary" as used in Sec. 48, must not be understood in its literal sense, i. e. things that cannot be done without. In such a sense none of the conveniences and apparatus found in schools would be necessary. I take it that all such things are necessary which in the judgment of the director would promote the efficiency and welfare of the school, having due regard to all the circumstances of the case.— *Kirchner, Atty. Gen., July 31, 1877.*

verified by the oath or affirmation of the person taking such census, by affidavit appended thereto or indorsed thereon, setting forth that it is a correct list of the names of all the children between the ages aforesaid residing in the district, which affidavit may be made before the clerk of the township; and said list shall be returned with the annual report of the director to the township clerk. Children in almshouses, prisons, or asylums, not otherwise residents of the district, and not attending the school, shall not be included in the said census; nor shall Indian children be so included unless they attend the school, or their parents are liable to pay taxes therein. *List to be filed with township clerk.* *What children not included.*

(§50.) SEC. 23. The directors shall also, at the end of the school year, and previous to the second Monday in September in each year, deliver to the township clerk, to be filed in his office, a report to the board of school inspectors of the township, showing: *To make annual reports to inspectors.*

First, The whole number of children belonging to the district between the ages of five and twenty years, according to the census taken as aforesaid; *Contents of.*

Second, The number attending school during the year under five, and also the number over twenty years of age;

Third, The number of non-resident pupils of the district that have attended school during the year;

Fourth, The whole number that have attended school during the year;

Fifth, The length of time the school has been taught during the year by a qualified teacher, the name of each teacher, the length of time taught by each, and the wages paid to each.

Sixth, The average length of time scholars, between five and twenty years of age, have attended school during the year;

Seventh, The amount of money received from the township treasurer apportioned to the district by the township clerk;

Eighth, The amount of money raised by the district, and the purposes for which it was raised;

Ninth, The kind of books used in the school;

Tenth, Such other facts and statistics in regard to the schools and the subject of education as the superintendent of public instruction shall direct.

(§51.) SEC. 24. The director of each fractional district shall make his annual report to the clerk of the township in which the school-house is situated, and shall also report to the clerk of each township in which the district is in part situated, the number of children between the ages of five and twenty years in that part of the district lying in such township. *Where director of fractional district to report.*

ASSESSOR.

(§52.) SEC. 25. It shall be the duty of the assessor of each school district: *Assessor. See App. A., ¶¶ 50, 66.*

(§52).—Is a district assessor justifiable under the law in refusing to pay an order drawn for any purpose not authorized by law although such order is duly signed by the director and countersigned by the moderator? Cases may arise in which the assessor is in duty bound not to pay such orders.—*Kirchner. Atty. Gen., May 22, 1860.*

First, To execute to the district and file with the director within ten days after his election or appointment a bond in double the amount of money to come into his hands as such assessor during his term of office, as near as the same can be ascertained, with two sufficient sureties, to be approved by the moderator and director, conditioned for the faithful application of all moneys that shall come into his hands by virtue of his office, and to perform all the duties of his said office as required by the provisions of this act. Said bond shall be filed with the director, and in case of any breach of the condition thereof, the moderator shall cause a suit to be commenced thereon in the name of the district, and any moneys collected thereon shall be paid into the township treasury, subject to the order of the district officers, and shall be applied to the same purposes as the moneys lost should have been applied by the assessor;

Second, To pay all orders of the director, when lawfully drawn and countersigned by the moderator, out of any moneys in his hands belonging to the fund upon which such orders may be drawn;

Third, To keep a book in which all the moneys received and disbursed shall be entered, the sources from which the same have been received, and the persons to whom and the objects for which the same have been paid;

Fourth, To present to the district board at the close of the school year a report in writing, containing a statement of all moneys received during the preceding year and of each item of disbursements made, and exhibit the voucher therefor;

Fifth, To appear for and on behalf of the district in all suits brought by or against the same, when no other directions shall be given by the qualified voters in district meeting, except in suits in which he is interested adversely to the district, and in all such cases the moderator shall appear for such district, if no other direction be given as aforesaid;

Sixth, At the close of his term of office to settle with the distrct board, and deliver to his successor in office all books, vouchers, orders, documents, and papers belonging to the office of assessor, together with all district moneys remaining on hand;

Seventh, To perform such other duties as are or shall be by law required of the assessor.

Margin notes:
- To give bond.
- See App. B., form 6.
- Bond to be approved.
- Bond filed with director.
- When suit to be brought thereon.
- To pay proper orders.
- To keep reccrd of receipts and disbursements.
- To make annua report to district board.
- To appear for district in suits.
- See App. A., ¶¶ 106, 109.
- To deliver to his successor books, papers, etc.
- Other duties.

(§52.) The sureties on a bond executed by the assessor of the school district are not responsible for acts or omissions occurring beyond the period for which the assessor was elected. In case of his re-election a new bond should be given.—*Kirchner Atty. Gen., Dec. 4, 1877.*

(§52.) Mr. S. was elected to the office of assessor of a school district and gave the requisite bonds. Since his first election he has been re-elected but has never executed any additional bonds. He has never been requested so to do by the moderator and director. Latterly the director requested him to execute an official bond and S. replied that he could not do so just then, and thereupon and without any further proceedings the district treated the office of assessor as vacant and proceeded at once to an election to fill said supposed vacancy. I am entirely clear that Mr. S. has not forfeited his office and that he is not only justified, but it is his duty not to pass over any of the papers pertaining to the office or any of the school district moneys. But Mr. S. should give bonds at once. Both the director and moderator were derelict in their duty in failing to require the bond of the assessor at the outset. After filing the bond Mr. S. should continue to administer the office of assessor.—*Kirchner, Atty. Gen., Sept. 18, 1879.*

CHAPTER IV.

TOWNSHIP OFFICERS.

TOWNSHIP BOARD OF SCHOOL INSPECTORS.

(§53.) SECTION 1. The school inspectors of each township, *Board of school inspectors.* together with the township clerk, shall constitute the township board of school inspectors. Said board shall meet within twenty *See §§ 141, 147.* days after the first Monday in April in each year, and elect one of their number, other than the township clerk, chairman of said board, and the township clerk shall be the clerk thereof.*

(§54.) SEC. 2. The chairman of said board shall be the treasurer *Chairman of board to be treasurer.* thereof, and shall give bond to the township in double the amount of moneys to come into his hands during his term of office, as *To give bond.* near as the same can be ascertained, with two sufficient sureties, to be approved by the township clerk, conditioned for the faithful *See App. B., form 13.* appropriation of all moneys that may come into his hands by virtue of his office. Said bond shall be filed with the township clerk, and *Bond to be filed.* in case of the non-fulfillment thereof, said clerk shall cause a suit *When suit to be brought thereon.* to be commenced thereon, and the moneys collected in such suit shall be paid into the township treasury, and shall be applied to the same purposes as the moneys lost should have been applied by said treasurer of the board of school inspectors.

(§55.) SEC. 3. On the third Monday in September in each *Inspectors to make triplicate report.* year, the inspectors shall make triplicate reports, setting forth the whole number of districts in their townships, the amount of money raised and received for township and district libraries, and such other items as shall from year to year be required by *Contents of.* the Superintendent of Public Instruction, together with the several particulars set forth in the reports of the school directors for the preceding year; and the township clerk shall, within ten *Disposition of reports.* days thereafter, forward two copies of the same to the secretary of the county board of school examiners, and file the other copy in his office.*

(§56.) SEC. 4. It shall be the duty of the school inspectors, *Inspectors to examine list of qualified teachers.* before making their annual report, as required by the preceding section, to examine the list of legally qualified teachers on file in the office of the township clerk, and if in any school district a *See § 134, Subd. 6.* school shall not have been taught for the time required by law during the preceding school year by a legally qualified teacher, no part of the public money shall be distributed to such district, *To report districts not employing such.* although the report from such district shall set forth that a school has been so taught ; and it shall be the duty of the board to certify to the facts in relation to any such district in their annual report.

---

*As amended by Act No. 9, session laws of 1883, and Act No. 96, session laws of 1885.
(§53.)—When the inspectors fail to elect a chairman within twenty days after the first Monday of April, I am of the opinion that the organization can be perfected after such date by the election of a chairman, and that failure to comply with the law referred to, does not preclude a legal organization thereafter.—*Taggart, Atty. Gen., May 20, 1886.*

* Amended by Act No. 266, Public Acts of 1887.

Inspectors to
render account
to township
board.

(§57.) SEC. 5. It shall be the duty of the board of inspectors to render to the township board, on the Tuesday next preceding the annual township meeting, a full and true account of all moneys received and disbursed by them as such inspectors during the year, which account shall be settled by said said township board, and such disbursements allowed, if the proper vouchers are presented.

Number of
meetings of
inspectors.

See App. A., § 1.

(§58.) SEC 6. The whole number of meetings of the township board of school inspectors at the expense of the township, during any one school year, shall not exceed eight; but this shall not be construed to prevent said board holding further meetings in case of necessity, provided no expense to the township be incurred.

TOWNSHIP CLERK.

Township clerk
to be clerk
of board of
inspectors.

Duties as such.

See §§ 141, 142.

(§ 59.) SEC. 7. The township clerk shall be the clerk of the board of school inspectors by virtue of his office, and shall attend all meetings of said board, and, under their direction, prepare all their reports and record the same, and shall record all their proceedings. He shall also receive and keep all reports to inspectors from the directors of the several school districts in his township, and all the books and papers belonging to the inspectors, and file such papers in his office; and he shall receive all such communications, blanks and documents as may be transmitted to him by the superintendent of public instruction, and dispose of the same in the manner directed by said superintendent.

To notify county
clerk of chair-
man of board
of inspectors.

(§60.) SEC. 8. It shall be the duty of the township clerk annually, immediately after the organization of the board of school inspectors of his township, to transmit to the county clerk a certified statement of the name and postofice address of the chairman of said board, and in case there shall be a change in such chairman, during the year, he shall immediately notify the county clerk of such change.

To make map
of districts.

Where map to
be filed.

When new map
to be made.

(§61.) SEC. 9. Each township clerk shall cause a map to be made of his township, showing by distinct lines thereon the boundaries of each school district, and parts of school districts therein, and shall regularly number the same thereon as established by the inspectors. One copy of such map shall be filed by the said clerk in his office, and the other copy he shall file with the supervisor of the township; and within one month after any division or alteration of a district, or the organization of a new one in his township, the said clerk shall file a new map and copy thereof as aforesaid, showing the same.

To report to
supervisor all
school taxes.

See § 145.

See App. D.,
form 22.

(§62.) SEC. 10. It shall be the duty of the township clerk of each township, on or before the first day of October of each year, to make and deliver to the supervisor of his township a certified copy of all statements on file in his office of moneys proposed to be raised by taxation in each of the several school districts of the township for school purposes. He shall also certify to the supervisor the amount to be assessed upon the taxable property of any school district retaining the district school-house or other property, on the division of the district, as the same shall have been determined by the inspectors, and he shall also certify the same to the director of such district, and to the director of the district entitled thereto.

(§63.) SEC. 11. On receiving notice from the county treasurer of the amount of school moneys apportioned to his township, the township clerk shall apportion the same amount to the several districts therein entitled to the same, in proportion to the number of children in each, between the ages of five and twenty years, as the same shall be shown by the annual report of the director of each district for the school year closing prior to the May apportionment.* _{To apportion school moneys received from county treasurer.}

<small>To apportion school moneys received from county treasurer.</small>

<small>See App. B., form 20.</small>

(§64.) SEC. 12. Said clerk shall also apportion to the school districts in his township, as required by law, on receiving notice of the amount from the township treasurer, all moneys raised by township tax, or received from other sources, for the support of schools; and in all cases make out and deliver to the township treasurer a written statement of the number of children in each district drawing money, and the amount apportioned to each district, and record the apportionment in his office; and whenever an apportionment of the primary school interest fund, or moneys raised by tax, or received from other sources, is made, he shall give notice of the amount to be received by each district to the director thereof.

<small>To apportion school taxes.</small>

<small>Statement to township treasurer.</small>

<small>See App. B., forms 20, 21.</small>

<small>To notify directors of amount apportioned districts.</small>

TOWNSHIP SUPERVISOR AND TREASURER.

(§65.) SEC. 13. It shall be the duty of the supervisor of the township to assess the taxes voted by every school district in his township, and also all other taxes provided for in this act, chargeable against such district or township, upon the taxable property of the district or township respectively, and to place the same on

<small>Assessment and collection of district taxes.</small>

<small>See § 145.</small>

*As amended by Act No. 92, Public Acts of 1887.

(§65.) A supervisor in levying school taxes erroneously included a part of the territory of one district in an adjoining district and when the tax was collected it was paid to the district in which the supervisor had included the territory in question, and not to the district in which the territory belonged. These proceedings on the part of the supervisor were clearly illegal, and the collection thereof could have been successfully resisted, or if the taxes had been paid under protest, the parties paying could have recovered the amount thus unlawfully collected. It has been held by the Supreme Court that acquiescence in and payment of an illegal tax, estops the taxpayer from afterwards complaining of it, but the payment of an illegal tax, if refused, cannot be enforced—(Wattles vs. City of Lapeer, 40 Mich., 625. The People ex. rel. Gebbart vs. East Saginaw, 30 Mich., 336). The taxes thus illegally assessed do not belong to either school district, therefore the one cannot sue the other for the recovery of such taxes improperly paid. It is not the money of the district in whose hands it now is, but it is an illegal tax collected from individuals, paid voluntarily and without protest and therefore cannot be collected back, for the Supreme Court in the case cited (40 Mich., 625), say: "If the people taxed acquiesce and pay these taxes they may not afterwards be heard to complain, but if they refuse, the courts have no power to compel them."—*Van Riper, Atty. Gen., July 24, 1882.*

(§65.) The only statute I notice relative to the assessment of school taxes is section 5000 Howell's Statutes, and subsequent sections. They are to be assessed upon the taxable property of the districts or township. I suppose the personal property of residents of the districts, together with the real estate of each resident within the district, would properly be taxed to each individual, notwithstanding the fact that some of his personal property was without the district and within the township. If the personalty was without the township and of that character to be assessable to another township another rule would apply. I do not think sections 10 and 11, Laws of 1885, applicable to school districts, or that they affect such taxes unless the property is in another township from where the party to be assessed resides.—*Taggart, Atty. Gen.*

the township assessment roll in the column for school taxes, and
the same shall be collected and returned by the township treasurer in the same manner and for the same compensation as town-

Taxes not
assessed at
proper time.

ship taxes. If any taxes provided for by law for school purposes
shall fail to be assessed at the proper time, the same shall be
assessed in the succeeding year.

Assessment of
one-mill tax.

(§66.) SEC. 14. The supervisor shall also assess upon the taxable property of his township one mill upon each dollar of the

How applied.

valuation thereof in each year, and report the aggregate valuation
of each district to the township clerk, who shall report said
amount to the director of each school district, in his township,
or to the director of any fractional school district, a portion of
which may be located in said township, before the first day of
September of each year, and all moneys so raised shall be apportioned by the township clerk to the district in which it was raised;

When forfeited
by districts.

and all money collected by virtue of this act during the year on
any property not included in any organized district, or in districts not having, during the previous school year, three months'
school in districts having less than thirty children, or five months'
school in districts having thirty and less than eight hundred
children, or nine months' school in districts having eight hun-

How appor-
tioned.

dred, or more children, as shown by the last school census, shall
be apportioned to the several other school districts of said township, in the same manner as the primary school interest fund is
now apportioned. All moneys accruing from the one mill tax in
any township, before any district shall have a legal school there-

Where accrued
moneys shall
belong.

in, shall belong to the district in which it was raised, when they
shall severally have had a three months' school by a qualified
teacher.*

When district is
divided certain
taxes to be
assessed.

(§67.) SEC. 15. The amount to be assessed upon the taxable
property of any school district retaining the school-house or other
property, on the division of a district, as the same shall have
been determined by the inspectors, shall be assessed by the supervisor in the same manner as if the same had been authorized by
a vote of such district; and the money so assessed shall be placed
to the credit of the taxable property taken from the former district, and shall be in reduction of any tax imposed in the new
district on said taxable property for school district purposes:

Proviso.

Provided, That if the district retaining the school-house shall
vote to pay, and shall pay, before said taxes are assessed, any
portion of said amount to the new district, said amount, as shall
be certified by the moderator and director of the new district to
the supervisor, shall be deducted from the amount to be assessed

How such taxes
to be applied.

as provided in this section. When collected, such amount shall
be paid over to the assessor of the new district, to be applied to
the use thereof in the same manner, under the direction of its
proper officers, as if such sum had been voted and raised by said
district for building a school-house or other district purposes.

Taxes in frac-
tional districts.

(§68.) SEC. 16. The full amount of all taxes to be levied upon the
taxable property in a fractional school district shall be certified

* As amended by Act No. 84, Public Acts of 1887.

by the district board to the township clerk of each township in
which such district is in part situated, and by such township
clerks to the supervisors of their respective townships, and it
shall be the duty of each of said supervisors to certify to each
other supervisor interested the amount of taxable property in
that part of the district lying in his township: *Provided*, That Proviso—how
when there exists a manifest difference in the valuation of prop- equalized.
erty assessed in fractional districts, composed of territory in
adjoining townships or counties, such valuation shall be equalized for this specific purpose by the supervisors of the townships
interested, at a joint meeting held for that purpose, on application of either of the supervisors of said townships. And such
supervisors shall respectively ascertain the proportion of such
taxes, including mill tax, to be placed on their respective assessment rolls, according to the amount of taxable poperty in each
part of such district. And if said supervisors cannot agree as to
the proportion of such taxes to be placed on their respective
assessment rolls, a supervisor from an adjoining township shall
be called to meet with said supervisors in said fractional district
and assist in equalizing said valuation. Said supervisor to be
paid at the rate of three dollars per diem for the time necessarily
employed in attendance at such meeting of the supervisors, and
all necessary traveling expenses, by the townships in interest.*

(§69.) SEC. 17. The supervisor, on delivery of the warrant for Statement
the collection of taxes to the township treasurer, shall also treasurer.
deliver to said treasurer, a written statement of the amount of
school and library taxes, the amount raised for district purposes
on the taxable property of each district in the township, the
amount belonging to any new district on the division of the
former district, and the names of all persons having judgments
assessed under the provisions of this act upon the taxable property
of any district, with the amount payable to such person on
account thereof.

(§70.) SEC. 18. The supervisor of each township, on the Statement to
delivery of the warrant for the collection of taxes to the town- urer of one-mill
ship treasurer, shall also deliver to said treasurer a written state- tax levied in
ment, certified by him, of the amount of the one-mill tax levied district.
upon any property lying within the bounds of a fractional school
district, a part of which is situate within his township, and the
returns of which are made to the clerk of some other township;
and the said township treasurer shall pay to the township treasurer of such other township the amount of the taxes so levied
and certified to him for the use of such fractional school district.

(§71.) SEC. 19. Whenever any portion of a school district Collection and
shall be set off and annexed to any other district, or organized of taxes on
into a new one, after a tax for district purposes other than the division of
payment of any debts of the district shall have been levied upon
the taxable property thereof, but not collected, such tax shall be
collected in the same manner as if no part of such district had

---

* As amended by Act No. 38, Public Acts of 1887, and Act No. 162, Public Acts of
1889.

GENERAL SCHOOL LAWS.

30

been set off, and the said former district, and the district to which the portion so set off may be annexed or the new district organized from such portion, shall each be entitled to such proportion of said tax as the amount of taxable property in each part thereof bears to the whole amount of taxable property on which such tax is levied.

All school taxes assessed to be paid next to township expenses.
See App. A, ¶¶ 35, 66, 78.
See App. B, form 19.

(§72.) SEC. 20. The township treasurer shall retain in his hands, out of the moneys collected by him, after deducting the amount of tax for township expenses, the full amount of the school taxes on the assessment roll, and hold the same subject to the warrant of the proper district officers, to the order of the school inspectors, or of the persons entitled thereto, and give a written notice to the township clerk of the amount.

Township treasurer to apply to county treasurer for moneys.
To notify township clerk of moneys.
Moneys due fractional districts.

(§73.) SEC. 21. The township treasurer shall, from time to time, apply to the county treasurer for all school and library moneys belonging to his township, or the districts thereof; and on receipt of the moneys to be apportioned to the districts, he shall notify the township clerk of the amount to be apportioned.

(§74.) SEC. 22. Each treasurer of a township, to the clerk of which the returns of any fractional school district shall be made, shall apply to the treasurer of any other township in which any part of such fractional school district may be situated, for any money to which such district may be entitled; and when so received it shall be certified to the township clerk, and apportioned in the same manner as other taxes for school purposes.

CHAPTER V.

COUNTY CLERK AND TREASURER.

County clerk to receive and dispose of communications, etc.

(§75.) SECTION 1. It shall be the duty of each county clerk to receive all such communications, blanks and documents as may be directed to him by the superintendent of public instruction, and dispose of the same in the manner directed by said superintendent.

County clerk to file inspectors' reports.
Notice of apportionment of moneys.

(§76.) SEC. 2. The clerk of each county shall, on receiving from the secretary of the county board of school examiners the annual reports of the several boards of school inspectors, file the same in his office. On receiving notice from the superintendent of Public Instruction of the amount of moneys apportioned to the several townships in his county, he shall file the same in his office, and forthwith deliver a copy thereof to the county treasurer.*

County treasurer to apply for moneys appropriated.
To notify township clerks of amounts.

(§77.) SEC. 3. The several county treasurers shall apply for and receive such moneys as shall have been apportioned to their respective counties, when the same shall become due; and each of said treasurers shall immediately give notice to the treasurer and clerk of each township in his county, of the amount of school moneys apportioned to his township, and shall hold the same subject to the order of the township treasurer.

*As amended by act No. 266, public acts of 1887.

CHAPTER VI.

(§78.) SECTION 1. Any school district may, by a two-thirds vote of the qualified electors of said district present at any annual meeting, or a special meeting called for that purpose borrow money, and may issue bonds of the district therefor, to pay for a school-house site or sites, and to erect and furnish school buildings as follows: Districts having less than thirty children between five and twenty years of age may have an indebtedness not to exceed three hundred dollars; districts having thirty children of like age may have an indebtedness not to exceed five hundred dollars; districts having fifty children of like age may have an indebtedness not to exceed one thousand dollars; districts having one hundred children of like age may have an indebtedness not to exceed three thousand dollars; districts having one hundred and twenty-five children of like age, and with an assessed valuation of not less than one hundred and fifty thousand dollars, may have an indebtedness not to exceed five thousand dollars; districts having two hundred children of like age may have an indebtedness not to exceed eight thousand dollars; districts having three hundred children of like age may have an indebtedness not to exceed fifteen thousand dollars; districts having four hundred children of like age may have an indebtedness not to exceed twenty thousand dollars; districts having five hundred children of like age may have an indebtedness not to exceed twenty-five thousand dollars; and districts having eight hundred children or more of like age may have an indebtedness not to exceed thirty thousand dollars: *Provided,* That the indebtedness of a district shall in no case extend beyond ten years for money borrowed: *Provided further,* That in all proceedings under this section the director, assessor, and one person appointed by the district board, shall constitute a board of inspection, who shall cause a poll-list to be kept, and a suitable ballot-box to be used, which shall be kept open two hours, and said ballotings shall be conducted in the same manner as at township elections.*

(§79.) SEC. 2. Whenever any school district shall have voted to borrow any sum of money, the district board of such district is hereby authorized to issue the bonds of such district, in such form, and executed in such manner by the moderator and director of such district, and in such sums, not less than fifty dollars, as such district board shall direct, and with such rate of interest, not exceeding eight per centum per annum, and payable at such time or times as the said district shall have directed.

Marginal notes: Districts may borrow money and issue bonds.— Amount limited.— Proviso—time for which bonds may be issued.— Proviso—regulations at elections to issue bonds.— Issuing bonds for money borrowed.— Interest thereon.

(878.) A school district has no power to issue bonds for purposes other than those enumerated in section 3726, compiled laws, as amended by act No. 173, laws of 1879 [i. e. to pay for a school-house site or sites, and to erect and furnish school buildings.] —*Kirchner, Attorney General, Nov. 5, 1880.*

* As amended by act No. 56, public acts of 1887.

Voters may raise tax to redeem bonds.

District may borrow money to pay bonds and issue further bonds.

Proviso.

(§80.) SEC. 3. Whenever any money shall have been borrowed by any school district, the taxable inhabitants of such district are hereby authorized at any regular meeting of such district, to impose a tax on the taxable property in such district, for the purpose of paying the principal thus borrowed, or any part thereof, and the interest thereon, to be levied and collected as other school district taxes are collected.

(§81.) SEC. 4. Any school district, whenever it shall appear that the same can be done on terms advantageous to said district, may borrow money to pay any bonded indebtedness of said district then existing, and issue further bonds of said district therefor: *Provided*, That a majority of the qualified voters of said district shall so determine, at an annual or special meeting called for that purpose; and that the notice of such meeting, whether annual or special, shall state the intention to take such vote.

CHAPTER VII.

SUITS AND JUDGMENTS AGAINST DISTRICTS.

See App. A., ¶¶ 97, 109.

Justices to have jurisdiction in certain cases.

(§82.) SECTION 1. Justices of the peace shall have jurisdiction in all cases of assumpsit, debt, covenant and trespass on the case against school districts, when the amount claimed, or matter in controversy shall not exceed one hundred dollars; and the parties shall have the same right of appeal as in other cases.

Suit against district, how commenced.

(§83.) SEC. 2. When any suit shall be brought against a school district, it shall be commenced by summons, a copy of which shall be left with the assessor of the district at least eight days before the return day thereof.

No execution to issue against district.

(§84.) SEC. 3. No execution shall issue on any judgment against a school district, nor shall any suit be brought thereon, but the same shall be collected in the manner prescribed in this act.

Assessor to certify to supervisor judgment against district.

(§85.) SEC. 4. Whenever any final judgment shall be obtained against a school district, if the same shall not be removed to any other court, the assessor of the district shall certify to the supervisor of the township and to the director of the district, the date and amount of such judgment, with the name of the person in whose favor the same was rendered, and if the judgment shall be removed to another court, the assessor shall certify the same as aforesaid, immediately after the final determination thereof against the district.

When assessor fails to certify, how party may proceed.

(§86.) SEC. 5. If the assessor shall fail to certify the judgment as required in the preceding section, it shall be lawful for the party obtaining the same, his executors, administrators or assigns to file with the supervisor the certificate of the justice or clerk of the court rendering the judgment showing the facts which should have been certified by the assessor.

How judgment certified in case of fractional district.

(§87.) SEC. 6. If the district against whom any such judgment shall be rendered is situated in part in two or more townships, a certificate thereof shall be delivered as aforesaid to the supervisor of each township in which such district is in part situated.

(§88.) SEC. 7. The supervisor or supervisors receiving either of the certificates of a judgment as aforesaid shall proceed to assess the amount thereof, with interest from the date of the judgment to the time when the warrant for the collection thereof will expire, upon the taxable property of the district, placing the same on the next township assessment roll in the column for school taxes; and the same proceedings shall be had, and the same shall be collected and returned in the same manner as other district taxes. Supervisors to assess amount of judgment. How collected and returned.

CHAPTER VIII.

SITES FOR SCHOOL-HOUSES.

(§89.) SECTION 1. The qualified voters of any school district, when lawfully assembled, may designate by a vote of two-thirds of those present, such number of sites as may be desired for school-houses, and may change the same by a similar vote at any annual meeting. When no site can be established by such inhabitants as aforesaid, the school inspectors of the township or townships in which the district is situated shall determine where such site shall be, and their determination shall be certified to the director of the district, and shall be final, subject to alteration afterward by the inspectors, on the written request of two-thirds of the qualified voters of the district, or by two-thirds of the qualified voters agreeing upon a site, at a district meeting lawfully called. See App. A., ¶¶ 114, 124. Voters to designate sites. When inspectors shall determine site. See App. B., form 17.

(§90.) SEC. 2. Whenever a site for a school-house shall be designated, determined, or established, in any manner provided by law, in any school district, and such district shall be unable to agree with the owner or owners of such site upon the compensation to be paid therefor, or in case such district shall, by reason of any imperfection in the title to said site, arising either from break in the chain of title, tax sale, mortgages, levies, or any other cause, be unable to procure a perfect, unincumbered title, in fee simple to said site, the district board of such district shall authorize one or more of its members to apply to the circuit judge, if there be one in the county, or to a circuit court commissioner of the county, or to any justice of the peace of the city or township in which such school district shall be situated, for a jury to ascertain and determine the just compensation to be made for the real estate required by such school district for such site, and the necessity for using the same, which application shall be in writing, and shall describe the real estate required by such district as accurately as is required in a conveyance of real estate : *Provided,* That whenever any school district shall have designated, selected, or established, in any manner provided by law, a school-house site, such selection, designation, or establishment shall be *prima fecie* evidence to said jury of the necessity to use the site so established. Disagreement upon compensation for site. Board to apply for a jury. Contents of application. Proviso—evidence of necessity for site.

Jury to be summoned.

(§91.) Sec. 3. It shall be the duty of such circuit judge, circuit court commissioner, or justice of the peace, upon such application being made to him, to issue a summons or *venire*, directed to the sheriff or any constable of the county, commanding him to summon eighteen freeholders residing in the vicinity of such site, who are in no wise of kin to the owner of such real estate, and not interested therein, to appear before such judge, commissioner, or justice, at the time and place therein named, not less than twenty nor more than fifty days from the time of issuing such summons or *venire*, as a jury to ascertain and determine the just compensation to be made for the real estate required by such school district for such site, and the necessity for using the

Owner to be notified.

same, and to notify the owner or occupant of such real estate, if he can be found in the county, of the time when and the place where such jury is summoned to appear, and the object for which such jury is summoned; which notice shall be served at least ten days before the time specified in such summons or *venire* for the jury to appear as hereinbefore mentioned.

Notice in case owner is unknown, etc.

(§92.) Sec. 4. Thirty days' previous notice of the time when and the place where such jury will assemble shall be given by the district board of such district, where the owner or owners of such real estate shall be unknown, non-residents of the county, minors, insane, *non compos mentis*, or inmates of any prison, by publishing the same in a newspaper published in the county where such real estate is situated; or if there be no newspaper published in such county, then in some newspaper published in the nearest county where a newspaper is published, once in each week for four successive weeks, which notice shall be signed by the district board or by the director or assessor of such district, and shall describe the real estate required for such site, and state the time when and place where such jury will assemble, and the object for which they will assemble; or such notice may be served on such owner personally, or by leaving a copy thereof at his last place of residence.

Return of venire and proceedings thereon.

(§93.) Sec. 5. It shall be the duty of such judge, commissioner, or justice, and of the persons summoned as jurors, as hereinbefore provided, and of the sheriff or constable summoning them to attend at the time and place specified in such summons or *venire*; and the officer who summoned the jury shall return such summons or *venire* to the officer who issued the same, with the names of the persons summoned by him as jurors, and shall certify the manner of notifying the owner or owners of such real estate, if he was found; and if he could not be found in said county, he shall certify that fact. Either party may challenge any of the said jurors for the same causes as in civil actions. If more than twelve of said jurors in attendance shall be found qualified to serve as jurors, the officer in attendance, and who issued the summons or *venire* for such jury, shall strike from the list of jurors a number sufficient to reduce the number of jurors in attendance to twelve; and in case less than twelve of the number so summoned as jurors shall attend, the sheriff or constable shall summon a sufficient number of freeholders to make up the number of twelve; and the officer issuing the summons or *venire* for such jury, may issue an attachment for any person summoned as a juror who shall fail to attend, and may enforce obedience to such summons, *venire*, or attachment, as courts of record, or justices' courts are authorized to do in civil cases. Attachment may issue to enforce obedience to process.

(§04.) SEC. 6. The twelve persons selected as the jury shall be duly sworn by the judge, commissioner, or justice in attendance, faithfully and impartially to inquire, ascertain and determine the just compensation to be made for the real estate required by such school district for such site, and the necessity for using the same in the manner proposed by such school district; and the persons thus sworn shall constitute the jury in such case. Subpœnas for witnesses may be issued, and their attendance compelled by such circuit judge, commissioner, or justice in the same manner as may be done by the circuit court or by a justice's court in civil cases. The jury may visit and examine the premises, and, from such examination and such other evidences as may be presented before them, shall ascertain and determine the necessity for using such real estate in the manner and for the purpose proposed by such school district, and the just compensation to be made therefor; and if such jury shall find that it is necessary that such real estate shall be used in the manner or for the purpose proposed by such school district, they shall sign a certificate in writing, stating that it is necessary that said real estate, describing it, should be used as a site for a school-house for such district; also stating the sum to be paid by such school district as the just compensation for the same. The said circuit judge, circuit court commissioner or justice of the peace, shall sign and attach to, and indorse upon the certificate thus subscribed by the said jurors, a certificate stating the time when and the place where the said jury assembled, that they were by him duly sworn as herein required, and that they subscribed the said certificate. He shall also state in such certificate who appeared for the respective parties on such hearing and inquiry, and shall deliver such certificates to the director, or to any member of the district board of such school district. Jury to be sworn. Subpœnas for witnesses. Jury to ascertain necessity for taking land. To determine compensation therefor. Court to make certificate.

(§95.) SEC. 7. Upon filing such certificates in the circuit court of the county where such real estate is situated, such court shall, if it finds all the proceedings regular, render judgment for the sum specified in the certificate signed by such jury, against such school district, which judgment shall be collected and paid in the manner as other judgments against school districts are collected and paid. Collection of judgment

(§96.) SEC. 8. In case the owner of such real estate shall be unknown, insane, *non compos mentis*, or an infant, or cannot be found within such county, it shall be lawful for the said school district to deposit the amount of such judgment with the county treasurer of such county, for the use of the person or persons entitled thereto; and it shall be the duty of such county treasurer When owner is unknown, etc., money to be deposited with county treasurer may be drawn.

to receive such money, and at the time of receiving it, to give a receipt or certificate to the person depositing the same with him,. stating the time when such deposit was made, and for what purpose; and such county treasurer and his sureties shall be liable on his bond for any money which shall come into his hands under the provisions of this act, in case he shall refuse to pay or account

Proviso—how money to be drawn from county treasurer.

for the same, as herein required: *Provided*, That no such money shall be drawn from such county treasurer, except upon an order of the circuit court, circuit court commissioner or judge of probate. as hereinafter provided.

On payment court to decree title vested in district.

(§97.) SEC. 9. Upon satisfactory evidence being presented to the circuit court of the county where such real estate lies, that such judgment, or the sum ascertained and determined by the jury as the just compensation to be paid by such district for such site, has been paid, or that the amount thereof has been deposited according to the provisions of the preceding sections, such court shall, by an order or decree, adjudge and determine that the title in fee of such real estate shall, from the time of making such payment or deposit, forever thereafter be vested in such school district and its successors and assigns, and shall, in and by such order or decree, award to such school district a writ of possession

Copy of decree to be recorded.

for the recovery of the possession of such real estate; a copy of which order or decree, certified by the clerk of said county, shall be recorded in the office of the register of deeds of such county, and the title of such real estate shall thenceforth, from the time of making such payment or deposit, be vested forever thereafter in such school district, and its successors and assigns in fee.

When district to take possession.

(§98.) SEC. 10. Such school district may, at any time after making payment or deposit hereinbefore required, enter upon and take possession of such real estate for the use of said district.

Writ of possession to be issued by county clerk to sheriff.

And it shall be the duty of the county clerk of said county, on the request of said school district, to issue out of and under the seal of the circuit court of said county a writ of possession as awarded in such order or decree; which writ shall be directed to the sheriff of said county, and shall be tested and made returnable, and shall be substantially, so far as may be, in the same form provided for writs of possession in actions of ejectment;.

Sheriff to remove respondent.

and it shall be the duty of such sheriff thereupon to remove the respondent or respondents in such proceedings, and all persons holding under them or either of them, from the real estate described in such decree and in such writ, and deliver the possession thereof with the appurtenances to such school district.

When jury disagrees proceedings may be adjourned and new jury summoned.

(§99.) SEC. 11. In case the jury hereinbefore provided for shall not agree, another jury may be summoned in the same manner, and the same proceedings may be had, except that no further notice of the proceedings shall be necessary; but instead of such notice, the judge, commissioner or justice may adjourn the proceedings to such time as he shall think reasonable, not exceeding thirty days, and shall make the process to summon a jury returnable at such time and place as the said proceedings shall be adjourned to. Such proceedings may be adjourned from time to time by the said judge, or commissioner, or justice, on the application of either party, and for good cause, to be shown by the party applying for such adjournment, unless the other party shall consent to such adjournment; but such adjournments shall not in all exceed three months. Adjournments not to exceed three months.

(§100.) SEC. 12. In case the said school-house site is encumbered by mortgage, levy, tax sale, or otherwise, as aforesaid, the mortgagee, or other parties claiming to be interested in said title shall severally be made a party to the procedure as aforesaid, and shall be authorized upon the filing of the certificate of the jury in the circuit court of said county, to appear before the circuit judge and make proof relative to their proportionate claims to the said site, or the compensation to be made therefor as determined by said jury. And the said circuit judge shall, by decree, settle their several claims in accordance with the rights of the parties respectively, and may divide the sum awarded by said jury between the claimants as in his judgment will be equitable and right, rendering against said district a separate judgment for each of the amounts so awarded. Proceedings in case of incumbrances. Duty of circuit judges.

(§101.) SEC. 13. The circuit judge, judge of probate, or circuit court commissioner of any county where any money has been deposited with the county treasurer of such county, as hereinbefore provided, shall, upon the written application of any person or persons entitled to such money, and upon receiving satisfactory evidence of the right of such applicant to the money thus deposited, make an order, directing the county treasurer to pay the money thus deposited with him to said applicant; and it shall be the duty of such county treasurer, on the presentation of such order, with the receipt of the person named therein indorsed on said order and duly acknowledged, in the same manner as conveyances of real estate are required to be acknowledged, to pay the same; and such order, with the receipt of the applicant or person in whose favor the same shall be drawn, shall, in all courts and places, be presumptive evidence in favor of such county treasurer, to exonerate him from all liability to any person or persons for said money thus paid by him. How money deposited with county treasurer may be drawn.

(§102.) SEC. 14. Circuit judges, circuit court commissioners, and justices of the peace, for any services rendered under the provisions of this act, shall be entitled to the same fees and compensation as for similar services in other special proceedings. Jurors, constables, and sheriffs shall be entitled to the same fees as for like services in civil cases in the circuit court. Compensation of officers, etc., on proceedings.

(§103.) SEC. 15. In case any circuit judge, circuit court commissioner, or justice of the peace, who shall issue a summons or *venire* for a jury, shall be unable to attend to any of the subsequent proceedings in such case, any other circuit court commissioner or justice of the peace may attend and finish said proceedings. When judge, etc., unable to attend, another may finish proceedings.

5

CHAPTER IX.

APPEALS FROM ACTION OF INSPECTORS.

See App. A., ¶¶ 5, 10.

When electors may appeal. (§104.) SECTION 1. Whenever any five or more tax-paying electors, having taxable property within any school district, shall feel themselves aggrieved by any action, order, or decision of the board of school inspectors, with reference to the formation, or any division, or consolidation of said school district, they may, at any time within sixty days from the time of such action on the part of said school inspectors, appeal from such action, order, or decision of said board of school inspectors to the township board of the township in which such school district is situated, **How made in fractional districts.** and in case of fractional school districts notice of such appeal shall be served on the clerk of the joint boards of school inspectors who have made the decision appealed from, who shall, within five days, give notice thereof to the township boards of the several townships in which the different parts of said fractional **Powers and duties of township board.** school district are situated, who shall have power, and whose duty it shall be, acting jointly, to entertain such appeal, and review, confirm, set aside, or amend the action, order, or decision of the board of school inspectors thus appealed from; or if in their opinion the appeal is frivolous or without sufficient cause, they may summarily dismiss the same.[f]

Appellants to file statement of cause. (§105.) SEC. 2. Said appellants shall, before taking such appeal, make out and file with the board of school inspectors, or in case of fractional school districts to the clerk of the joint boards of school inspectors, a written statement, to be signed by said appellants, setting forth in general terms the action, order, or decision of the board or boards of school inspectors with respect to which the appellants feel themselves aggrieved, and their demand for an appeal therefrom to the township board or boards of said town- **Appellants to execute bond.** ship or townships, and shall also cause to be executed and signed by one of their number, and by two good and sufficient sureties to be approved by the clerk of said board or joint boards of school inspectors or by any justice of the peace of the township, and **Where filed.** filed with the clerk of said board or joint boards of school inspectors, a bond to the people of the State of Michigan in the penal sum of two hundred dollars, conditioned for the due prosecution of said appeal before said township board or boards acting jointly, and also, in case of the dismissal of said appeal as frivolous by said township board or joint boards, for the payment by said appellants of all costs occasioned to the township or townships by reason of said appeal.[s]

Duty of inspectors when appeal is filed. (§106.) SEC. 3. Upon the filing of such appeal papers and bond with the said board or joint boards of school inspectors, the said board or joint boards of school inspectors shall, within ten days thereafter, make out and file with the clerk of said township in

---

[f] As amended by Act No. 82, Session Laws 1883.
[s] As amended by Act No. 82, Session Laws of 1883.

which the said school-house is located, a full and complete transcript of all their proceedings, actions, orders, or decisions with reference to which the appeal is taken, and of their records of the same; also said bond and appeal papers, and all petitions and remonstrances, if any, with reference to the matters appealed from; and upon the filing of the same with the said township clerk, the said township board or boards shall be deemed to be in possession of the case, and if the return be deemed by them insufficient, may order a further and more complete return by said board or boards of school inspectors; and when such return shall by them be deemed sufficient, they shall proceed with the consideration of the appeal, at such time or times, within ten days after such return, and in such manner and under such affirmation, amendment or reversal of the action, order, or decision of the board or boards of school inspectors appealed from, as in their judgment shall seem to be just and right; or, they deem the appeal to be frivolous, they may summarily dismiss the same; but the decision of said board or boards of school inspectors shall not be altered or reversed, unless a majority of such township board or boards, not members of said board or boards of school inspectors, shall so determine.

When township board deemed in possession of case.

Proceedings in the appeal.

When members of township board cannot act in determining case.

See App. A., ¶¶ 14, 15.

CHAPTER X.

GRADED SCHOOL DISTRICTS.

(§107.) SECTION 1. Any school district containing more than one hundred children between the ages of five and twenty years may, by a two-thirds vote of the qualified electors present at any annual or special meeting, organize as a graded school district: *Provided*, That the intention to take such vote shall be expressed in the notice of such annual or special meeting. When such change in the organization of the district shall have been voted, the voters at such annual or special meeting shall proceed immediately to elect by ballot from the qualified voters of the district one trustee for the term of one year, two for the term of two years, and two for a term of three years, and annually thereafter a successor or successors to the trustee or trustees

See App. A., ¶¶ 135, 143.

What districts may organize as such.

Proviso—notice of meeting.

Election of trustees.

Term of office.

(§107.) Elections held in graded school districts wherein two trustees were balloted for at the same time, on joint ballot, are void, and no person has been legally elected. It has frequently been held that, if a ballot contains the names of two persons for the same office, when but one is to be chosen, it is bad as to both. The election of two trustees on two separate ballots, would be good as to the first one chosen, and void as to the second. As it is the policy of the law to uphold elections where the choice of the people can be ascertained, the one first elected having received the necessary vote is the choice of the electors, and such action of the district is valid as to him. As the amendment of 1883 does not repeal section 1, act X, only so far as it is in conflict therewith, and as both statutes provide that trustees shall hold over until their successors shall be elected and qualified, the old board remain in office until a valid election is had. The law makes no provision for a special election for trustees of graded schools, hence where the regular election was void there can be no special election to fill the office. No election can be held without a law providing therefor, hence the law that both trustees hold over is in full force wherever there was a failure to elect, as provided by statute. Section 2, chapter 3, of the school law applies only to officers of district schools, and not to trustees of graded schools, and only permits a special election where two vacancies exist. The trustees have no power under section 2, chapter X, to appoint a trustee where there has been a failure to elect, but can only fill vacancies, as in case of death, resignation or removal.—*Van Riper, Atty. Gen., July 26, 1883.*

Proviso.	whose term of office shall expire: *Provided also*, In all districts organized prior to the year eighteen hundred and eighty-three there shall be one trustee elected at the annual meeting for the year eighteen hundred and eighty-three, and thereafter there shall be elected a trustee or trustees in the manner aforesaid, whose term of office shall be three years, and until his or their successor or successors shall have been elected and filed his or their
Majority vote necessary to elect.	acceptance: *Provided also*, That in the election of trustees, and all other school officers, the person receiving a majority of all the votes shall be declared elected.[b]
Acceptance of office to be filed. See App. B., form 5. Officers to be elected by trustees.	(§108.) SEC. 2. Within ten days after their election such trustees shall file with the director acceptances of the offices to which they have been elected, and shall annually elect from their own number a moderator, a director, and assessor, and for cause may remove the same, and may appoint others of their own number in their places, who shall perform the duties prescribed by law for such officers in other school districts in this State, except
Vacancy in board, how filled. When inspectors shall appoint officers. See App. B., form 15.	as herinafter provided. The trustees shall have power to fill any vacancy that may occur in their number till the next annual meeting. Whenever, in any case, the trustees shall fail, through disagreement or neglect, to elect the officers named in this section, within twenty days next after the annual meeting, the school inspectors of the township or city to which such district makes its annual report snall appoint the said officers from the number of said trustees.
Duty of trustees.	(§109.) SEC. 3. It shall be the duty of the board of trustees of any graded school district:
To classify pupils.	*First*, To classify and grade the pupils attending school in such district, and cause them to be taught in such schools or departments as they may deem expedient;
To establish high schools, etc. See App. A., ¶¶ 142, 143.	*Second*, To establish in such district a high school when ordered by a vote of the district at an annual meeting, and to determine the qualifications for admission to such school, and the fees to be paid for tuition in any branches taught therein;
To audit and pay director's accounts.	*Third*, To audit and order the payment of all accounts of the director for incidental or other expenses incurred by him in the discharge of his duties; but no more than fifty dollars shall be expended by the director in any one year for repairs of the buildings or appurtenances of the district property without the authority of the board of trustees;
To employ teachers. See § 40. See App. B., form 26.	*Fourth*, To employ all qualified teachers necessary for the several schools, and to determine the amount of their compensation, and to require the director and moderator to make contracts with

[b] As amended by Act No. 28, Session Laws 1883, and Act No. 18, Session Laws 1885.

(§ 109, paragraph four.) The question is as to whether the board of trustees of a graded school can employ a music teacher who has not passed the regular examination required of other teachers and received a certificate required by section 5153 of Howell's Statutes (Sec. 4, Chap. 11, School Laws)? It would be most difficult to imagine that an examination in the several branches and studies specified in the statutes would show sufficiently the qualifications of the applicants to teach either music or drawing. I do not think the statute applicable to such teachers nor does there appear to be any which is. The board probably has and will be held by the courts to possess such authority, still it is not a question free from doubt and additional legislation may be desirable.—*Taggart, Attorney General, July 26, 1886.*

the same on behalf of the district, in accordance with the pro- ^{See App. A.,} visions of law concerning contracts with teachers; ¶¶ 79-86.

Fifth, To employ such officers and servants as may be neces- To employ sary for the management of the schools and school property, and officers, etc. prescribe their duties and fix their compensation;

Sixth, To perform such other duties as are required of district Other duties. boards in other school districts. See Chap. III.

(§110.) SEC. 4. No alteration shall be made in the boundaries Consent of trus- of any graded school district, without the consent of a majority tees necessary to change in of the trustees of said district, which consent shall be spread upon boundaries of the records of the district, and placed on file in the office of the districts. clerk of the board of school inspectors of the township or city to which the reports of said district are made; and graded school Such districts districts shall not be restricted to nine sections of land. in size.

(§111.) SEC. 5. Whenever two or more contiguous districts hav- Two or more districts can ing together more than one hundred children betwen the ages of unite and form five and twenty years, after having published in the notices of the district. annual meetings of each district the intention to take such action, shall severally, by a vote of two-thirds of the qualified voters attending the annual meeetings in said districts, determine to unite for the purpose of establishing a graded school district under the provisions of this chapter, the school inspectors of the township or townships in which such districts may be situated shall, on being properly notified of such vote, proceed to unite such districts, and shall appoint, as soon as practicable, a time and place for a meeting of the new district, and shall require Notice of meeting. three notices of the same to be posted in each of the districts so united at least five days before the time of such meeting, and at such meeting the district shall elect a board of trustees, as pro- vided in section one of this chapter, and may do whatever busi- ness may be done at any annual meeting.[1]

CHAPTER XI.

LIBRARIES.

(§112.) SECTION 1. A township library shall be maintained in Township libraries to be each organized township, which shall be the property of the maintained. township, and shall not be subject to sale or alienation from any + cause whatever. All actions relating to such library, or for the recovery of any penalties lawfully established in relation thereto, shall be brought in the name of the township.

(§113.) SEC. 2. All persons who are residents of the township Who are entitled to privileges of shall be entitled to the privileges of the township library, subject library. to such rules and regulations as may be lawfully established in relation thereto: *Provided,* That persons residing within the Proviso. boundaries of any school district in which a district library has been established shall be entitled to the privileges of such dis- trict library only.

[1] New section added by Act No. 53, Session Laws of 1883.

Inspectors to have charge.

See App B., form 18.

See App. A., ¶¶ 144, 140.

(§114.) SEC. 3. The township board of school inspectors shall have charge of the township library, and shall apply for and receive from the township treasurer all moneys appropriated for the township library of their township, and shall purchase the books and procure the necessary appendages for such library.

Inspectors accountable for care, etc., of library.

Powers of inspectors.

See App. C.

(§115.) SEC. 4. Said board shall be held accountable for the proper care and preservation of the township library, and shall have power to provide for the safe keeping of the same, to prescribe the time for taking and returning books, to assess and collect fines and penalties for the loss or injury of said books, and to establish all other needful rules and regulations for the management of the library, as said board shall deem proper, or the superintendent of public instruction may advise.

Where library to be kept.

Librarian.

(§116.) SEC. 5. The board of school inspectors shall cause the township library to be kept at some central or eligible place in the township, which it shall determine; such board shall also, within ten days after the annual township meeting, appoint a librarian for the term of one year, to have the care and superintendence of said library, who shall be responsible to the board of school inspectors for the impartial enforcement of all rules and regulations lawfully established in relation to said library.ʲ

What districts may establish libraries.

(§117.) SEC. 6. Any school district having a school census of not less than one hundred children, by a two-thirds vote at any annual meeting, may establish a district library, and such district shall be entitled to its just proportion of books from the library of any township in which it is wholly or partly situated, to be added to the district library, and also to its equitable share of any library moneys remaining unexpended in any such township or townships at the time of the establishment of such district library, or that shall thereafter be raised by tax in such township or townships, or that shall thereafter be apportioned to the township to the inspectors of which the annual report of its director is made.

District board to have charge of district library.

(§118.) SEC. 7. The district board of any school district in which a district library may be established in accordance with the provisions of this act shall have charge of such library; and the duties and responsibilities of said district board in relation to the district library, and all moneys raised or apportioned for its support, shall be the same as those of the board of school inspectors are to the township library.

Inspectors to report library statistics to State superintendent.

(§119.) SEC. 8. The school inspectors shall give in their annual report to the superintendent of public instruction, such facts and statistics relative to the management of the township library and the library moneys, as the superintendent of public instruction shall direct; and the district board of any school district having a library, shall cause to be given in the annual report of the director to the board of school inspectors, like facts and statistics relative to the district library, which items shall also be included by the said inspectors in their annual report.

As amended by Act No. 114, Session Laws of 1883.

(§120.) SEC. 9. In case the board of school inspectors of any township, or the district board of any school district, shall fail to make the report required by the preceding section, or in case it shall appear from the reports so made that any township or school district has failed to use the library money in strict accordance with the provisions of law, such township or district shall forfeit its share of the library moneys that are apportioned, and the same shall be apportioned to the several other townships and districts in the county as hereinafter provided: *Provided,* that in townships where the boards thereof shall determine and report to the superintendent that the public will be better served by using the said money for general school purposes, no such forfeiture shall occur.

Failure to report or illegal use of moneys to cause forfeiture of moneys thereafter.

Proviso.

(§121.) SEC. 10. The superintendent of public instruction shall annually and previous to the tenth day of May, transmit to the clerk of each county a statement of the townships in his county that are entitled to receive library moneys, giving the number of children in each of such townships between the ages of five and twenty years, as shall appear from the reports of the boards of school inspectors for the school year last ending; said clerk shall file such statement in his office, and shall forthwith furnish a copy thereof to the county treasurer.

State superintendent to provide county clerk with statement.

Statement to be filed and copy given to county treasurer.

(§122.) SEC. 11. The clear proceeds of all fines for any breach of the penal laws of this State and for penalties, or upon any recognizances in criminal proceedings, and all equivalents for exemptions [exemption] from military duty when collected in any county and paid into the county treasury, together with all moneys heretofore collected and paid into said treasury on account of such fines or equivalents, and not already appropriated [apportioned], shall be apportioned by the county treasurer before the first day of June in each year, among the several townships in the county, according to the number of children therein, between the ages of five and twenty years, as shown by the statement of the superintendent of public instruction provided for in the preceding section, which money shall be exclusively applied to the support of the township and district libraries, and to no other purpose: *Provided,* That from and after January first, one thousand eight hundred and eighty-two, such money may be used for general school purposes in any township wherein the township board thereof shall so determine.

Apportionment of proceeds of penal fines.

See App. A., ¶ 146.

How applied.

Proviso.

(§123.) SEC. 12. The qualified voters of each township shall have power, at any annual township meeting, to vote a tax for the support of libraries established in accordance with the provisions of this act, and the qualified voters of any school district, in which a district library shall be established, shall have power, at any annual meeting of such district, to vote a district tax for

Voters may levy tax for support of libraries.

(§121.) I am clearly of the opinion that the superintendent could make his report at any time before the first day of June, and that it would be the duty of the clerk to forward the same to the county treasurer, and that it would be his duty to make the apportionment, even if delayed beyond the time fixed by law. This, however, is with the superintendent, and it must be a very exceptional case that would justify him in a failure to comply with the clearly expressed provisions of law.

How tax to be reported, assessed, and collected.

the support of said district library. When any tax authorized by this section shall have been voted, it shall be reported to the supervisor, levied, and collected in the same manner as other township and school district taxes.

District board may give or sell books to township library.

(§124.) SEC. 13. The district board of any school district may donate or sell any library book or books belonging to such district to the board of school inspectors of the township or townships in which said district is wholly or partly situated, which book or books shall thereafter form a part of the township library.

CHAPTER XII.

EXAMINATION OF TEACHERS AND SUPERVISION OF SCHOOLS.

Election of school examiners.

Term of office.

Proviso.

Duties of county clerk in relation to election, etc.

Oath of examiner to be filed.

Election of secretary of board.

(§125.) SECTION. 1. The chairmen of the boards of school inspectors of the several townships in each county shall meet at the office of the county clerk of their county on the first Tuesday in August, in each year, and elect by ballot one school examiner, who shall hold his office for two years, or until his successor shall have been duly elected and qualified : *Provided*, That in the year eighteen hundred and eighty-seven there shall be no election of examiner, but the two examiners previously elected whose terms of office shall not have expired shall hold for the unexpired portions of the terms for which they were elected. The county clerk shall be the clerk of such elections in all cases, and in case of a tie shall give the casting vote, and he shall preserve a record of such election in a book to be kept for that purpose, and shall immediately after such election notify the person so elected of his election. The school examiners shall, within ten days after receiving notice of their election, take and subscribe the constitutional oath of office, the same to be filed with the county clerk, and shall enter upon the duties of their offices on the fourth Tuesday of August following their election.[k]

(§126.) SEC. 2. The two school examiners elected by the township chairmen shall meet at the office of the judge of probate of the county on the fourth Tuesday of August of each year, and with the judge of probate, who shall act as a member and clerk

---

(§125.) The county examiner will not lose his residence or forfeit his office, by reason of the temporary removal of his family into another city or village, provided such absence is merely temporary, and the intent is to return as soon as the education of his children in the university or college is accomplished. It is the intent of the party that governs, and a man's temporary absence in another State or foreign country even for a period of years, does not change his legal domicile, provided, as before stated, that he does not relinquish his home in the one place and take it up in the other place with intent to remain in such new home.—*VanRiper, Attorney General, June 23, 1882.*

(§125.) I am of the opinion that an election of school examiner by less than a majority is not a valid election and a person elected by less than a majority is not legally elected and cannot claim to hold such office.—*VanRiper, Attorney General, Aug. 28, 1882.*

(§126.) It is made the duty of the two school examiners with the judge of probate acting as a member and clerk of the board, to employ a secretary. I do not think it was the intention of the Legislature that they should employ one of their own members as secretary; if such were the intent it would have been so expressed, as in the old law. Independent of statute the rule is pretty well settled by the courts that an official cannot, by his own vote, elect himself to any position.—*Taggart, Attorney General, Sept. 2, 1887.*

of the board for the purpose herein named, shall elect, appoint and employ a secretary of said board of examiners. The judge of probate shall, immediately after the board has appointed a secretary, file a certified statement of such fact with the county clerk, and said county clerk shall immediately notify the person *Duty of county clerk.* appointed as secretary of his appointment, and said secretary shall, within ten days after receiving notice of his appointment, take and subscribe the constitutional oath of office, the same to be filed with the county clerk. He shall also execute a bond with *Secretary to execute bond.* two sufficient sureties, to be approved by and filed with the county clerk, in the penal sum of five hundred dollars, conditioned that he will faithfully discharge his duties according to law, and faithfully account for and pay over to the proper persons all moneys which may come into his hands by reason of his holding such office; and thereupon the county clerk shall report the name and postoffice address of such secretary to the superintendent of public instruction, and said secretary shall immediately thereafter enter upon the duties of his office. The secretary of the board shall be *ex officio* a member and the executive officer of the board of examiners in the transaction of all business of said board, except in the appointing or removing from office of the secretary of said board. The school examiner elected by the township *Chairman of board.* chairman, whose term of office shall soonest expire, shall be the chairman of the board of examiners.[k]

(§127.) SEC. 3. The secretary of the board of school examiners, *Public examination of teachers.* for the purpose of examining all persons who may offer themselves as teachers for the public schools, shall hold two regular public examinations in each, year at the county seat, which examinations shall be on the first Thursday of March and August; for a like purpose, said secretary shall hold not to exceed six *Special examinations.* special public examinations at such times and places as in the judgment of said board of examiners, the interest of the schools and teachers of the county shall require: *Provided,* That first and second grade certificates shall be granted only at the regular public examinations provided for in this section: *Provided, further,* That it shall be the duty of the secretary of the board *Schedule to be made and published.* of school examiners to make out a schedule of the times and places of holding special examinations, and to cause it to be published in one or more newspapers of the county at least ten days before each special examination, and he shall send a copy thereof to the chairman of each township board of school inspectors of the county, at least ten days previous to the time of holding any special examination.[k]

(§128.) SEC. 4. The board of school examiners shall meet on *Certificates, to whom granted.* the Saturday following each public examination held by the secretary, and shall grant certificates to teachers in such form as the superintendent of public instruction shall prescribe, licensing as teachers all persons who shall have attained the age of sixteen years, who have attended said public examination and

---

k As amended by Act No. 266, Public Acts of 1887.

who shall be found qualified in respect to good moral character, learning and ability to instruct and govern a school; but no certificate shall be granted to any person who shall not pass a satisfactory examination in orthography, reading, writing, grammar, geography, arithmetic, theory and art of teaching, United States history, civil government, and physiology and hygiene with particular reference to the effects of alcoholic drinks, stimulants, and narcotics upon the human system. All certificates shall be signed by the secretary and chairman of said board.

None but legally qualified teachers to be employed. No person shall be considered a qualified teacher within the meaning of the school law, nor shall any school officer employ or contract with any person to teach in any of the public schools who has not a certificate in force granted by the board of school examiners of the county or other lawful authority: *Provided,*

Questions for examination to be furnished by superintendent of public instruction. That all examination questions shall be prepared and furnished by the superintendent of public instruction to said secretary under seal, to be opened before the applicants for certificates on the day of examination.[k]

Grades of certificates. (§129.) SEC. 5. There shall be three grades of certificates granted by the board of school examiners in its discretion, and subject to such rules and regulations as the superintendent of public instruction may prescribe, which grades of certificates shall be as follows:

First. The certificate of the first grade shall be granted only to those who shall have taught at least one year with ability and success, and it shall be valid throughout the State for three years: *Provided,* That no first grade certificate shall be valid in any county other than that in which it was issued, unless a copy of said certificate is filed with the secretary of the county board of examiners in the county in which the holder of said certificate desires to teach.

Second. The certificate of the second grade shall be granted only to those who shall have taught at least six months with ability and success, and it shall be valid throughout the county for which it shall be granted for two

Third. years. The certificate of the third grade shall license the holder thereof to teach in the county for which it shall be granted for

Proviso—special certificates. **See App. A., ¶ 95.** one year: *Provided,* That the secretary of the board of school examiners or any other member of the board authorized by said secretary shall have power, upon personal examination satisfactory to himself, and subject to such rules and regulations as the board of school examiners may establish, to grant special certificates, which shall license the holder thereof to teach in a specified

Limit of special certificates. district for which it shall be granted; but such certificate shall not continue in force beyond the time of the next public examination and it shall not in any way exempt the teacher from a full

Second special certificate not to be granted without consent of the board. examination: *Provided, further,* That in case the holder of a special certificate does not appear for examination before the board at the next public examination succeeding the date of such special certificate, a second special certificate shall not be granted to such person except by order of the board of examiners, nor shall any member of the board of examiners, unless authorized by the board, grant a special certificate to any person who at a previous examination failed to secure a certificate.[k]

(§130.) SEC. 6. The board of school examiners may suspend or revoke any teacher's certificate for any reason which would have justified said board in withholding the same when given—for neglect of duty, for incompetency to instruct or govern a school, or for immorality; and said board may, within its jurisdiction, suspend, for immorality or incompetency to instruct and govern a school, the effect of any teacher's certificate that may have been granted by other lawful authority: *Provided*, That no certificate shall be suspended or revoked without a personal hearing, unless the holder thereof shall, after reasonable notice, neglect or refuse to appear before the board of school examiners for that purpose.[k] *[margin: Suspension or revocation of certificates.]* *[margin: Proviso.]*

(§131.) SEC. 7. It shall be the duty of the board of school examiners and the chairman [chairmen] of the board [boards] of school inspectors of the several townships to hold each year a joint meeting at the county seat at the time of and immediately after the annual election of school examiners, for the purpose of consulting and advising with reference to the more efficient supervision of the schools and teachers under their charge. The chairman of the board of school examiners shall preside at such joint meeting, and the secretary of the board of school examiners shall be secretary of such meeting.[k] *[margin: Examiners and inspectors to hold joint meetings yearly.]*

(§132.) SEC. 8. Special meetings of the board of school examiners may be called by the secretary of said board, as hereinafter provided, and at any meeting of the board of school examiners any two members thereof may transact any business that may lawfully come before such meeting. In case the secretary be not present at any meeting of the board, the examiner, acting as secretary, shall certify to the secretary a correct record of the proceedings, and the result of examinations at such meeting.[k] *[margin: Special meetings of board of examiners.]*

(§133.) SEC. 9. It shall be the duty of the secretary of the board of school examiners: *[margin: Duties of secretary.]*

First, Immediately upon his qualification as secretary, to send notice thereof to the superintendent of public instruction, and to the chairman of each township board of school inspectors of the county; *[margin: To send notice of his election.]*

Second, To be present at all meetings of the board, and to keep a record of all proceedings of the board; *[margin: To keep records of board.]*

Third, To keep a record of all examinations held by the board, and to sign all certificates and other papers and reports issued by said board; *[margin: To sign certificates, etc.]*

Fourth, To act as treasurer of the board for the purpose of receiving the institute fees provided by law, and paying the same to the county treasurer once in each month; *[margin: To act as treasurer of board.]*

Fifth, To keep a record of all certificates granted, suspended or revoked by the board, showing to whom issued, together with the date, grade and duration of each certificate, and if suspended or revoked, the date and reason therefor; *[margin: To keep record of certificates.]*

[k] As amended by Act No. 266, Public Acts of 1887.

Sixth, To furnish, previous to the first Monday in September in each year, to the township clerk of each township in the county, a list of all persons legally authorized to teach in the county at large, and in such township, with the date and term of each certificate, and if any have been suspended or revoked, the date of such suspension or revocation;

Seventh, To visit each of the schools in his county at least once each year, and to examine carefully the discipline, the mode of instruction, and the progress and proficiency of the pupils: *Provided,* That in case the secretary is unable to visit all the schools of the county, as herein required, he may, with the approval of the other members of the board of examiners, appoint such assistant visitors as may be necessary, who shall perform such duties pertaining to the visitation and supervision of schools as said secretary shall direct;

Eighth, To counsel with the teachers and school boards as to the courses of study to be pursued, and as to any improvement in discipline and instruction in the schools;

Ninth, To note the condition of the school-houses and the appurtenances thereto, and to suggest plans for new houses to be erected, and for warming and ventilating the same, and for the general improvement of school-houses and grounds;

Tenth, To promote by such means as he may devise, subject to the advice of the board of school examiners, the improvement of the schools in his county and the elevation of the character and qualifications of the teachers and officers thereof;

Eleventh, To receive the duplicate annual reports of the several boards of school inspectors, examine into the correctness of the same, requiring them to be amended when necessary, indorse his approval upon them and immediately thereafter, and before the first day of November in each year, transmit to the superintendent of public instruction one copy of each of said reports and file the other copy in the office of the county clerk;

Twelfth, To be subject to such instructions and rules as the superintendent of public instruction may prescribe; to receive all blanks and communications that may be sent to him by the superintendent of public instruction, and to dispose of the same as directed by the said superintendent; and to make annual reports at the close of the school year to the superintendent of public instruction, of the official labor performed by the board of school examiners, and by himself and of the general condition and management of the schools of the county, together with such other information as may be required of him;

Thirteenth, To perform such other duties as may be required of him by law, or the board of school examiners, and at the close of his term of office, to deliver all records, books and papers belonging to his office to the board of examiners.[x]

(§134.) Sec. 10. It shall be the duty of the chairman of the board of school inspectors of each township:

Marginal notes:
- To furnish list of qualified teachers to township clerks.
- To visit each school in county.
- To appoint assistant visitors when necessary.
- To counsel with teachers, etc.
- To suggest plans for school-houses.
- To advance the interests of schools.
- To examine inspectors' reports.
- To make annual report.
- Duties of chairman of board of school inspectors.

[x] As amended by Act No. 266, Public Acts of 1887.

First, To have general supervisory charge of the schools of his township, subject to such advice and direction as the secretary of the county board of examiners may give;

Second, To notify the secretary of the board of school examiners of any school within his township that is not being conducted in a successful and profitable manner;

Third, To make such reports of his official labors, and the condition of the schools as the superintendent of public instruction may direct, or the board of school examiners request;

Fourth, To perform such other duties as may be required of him by law, or that the superintendent of public instruction may direct.ᵡ

(§135.) Sec. 11. Each member of the board of school examiners, other than the secretary, shall receive four dollars for each day actually employed in the duties of his office. The compensation of the secretary of the board of examiners shall be determined by the board appointing him, as provided for in section two of this act: *Provided,* In counties having thirty districts or less such compensation shall not exceed three hundred dollars per annum; in counties having more than thirty districts such compensation shall be not to exceed at the rate of ten dollars for each district coming under the provisions of this act; but in no case shall the salary of the secretary of the board of examiners be more than fifteen hundred dollars per annum. The compensation of any assistant visitor, when appointed as provided in this act, shall be determined by the board of school examiners, but in no case shall it exceed three dollars for each day: *Provided,* That the number of days so employed shall not exceed thirty in any one year, necessarily devoted to the duties required of him. The compensation of each member of the board of school examiners, including the secretary and any assistant visitor, shall be paid quarterly from the county treasury, upon such member filing with the county clerk a sworn statement of his account, signed by the chairman and secretary of the board of school examiners, and obtaining an order from the county clerk upon the county treasurer for the amount of such account: *Provided,* That in no case shall the secretary of the board of examiners receive any order for his compensation from the county clerk until he has filed a certified statement from the superintendent of public instruction that all required reports have been properly made and filed with said superintendent. The necessary contingent expenses of the board of examiners for printing, postage, stationery, record books and rent of rooms for public examinations, shall be audited and allowed by the board of supervisors of the county, but shall in no county exceed the sum of two hundred dollars per annum, but no traveling fees shall be allowed to the secretary or any member of the board of examiners or to any assistant visitor. The compensation of the several chairmen of the township board of school inspectors, when in attendance at the annual meeting for the election of school examiners and the annual joint meeting with the board of school examiners, shall be the

[marginal notes:] Compensation of examiners. Compensation of secretary. Proviso—compensation limited. How paid. Proviso—statement from superintendent of public instruction necessary. Contingent expenses. Compensation of chairmen of boards of inspectors.

same as is allowed to members of the board of supervisors of the county, and when performing other duties required of him, as provided in this act, the same as is allowed to school inspectors by law: *Provided,* Said chairman shall not receive to exceed two dollars for each school district in the township, the same to be audited by the township boards of their respective townships and paid as other expenses of the township.[k]

Removal of examiners from office.

Removal of secretary.

(§136.) SEC. 12. Any member of a board of school examiners, other than the secretary, may be removed from office by the judge of probate of the county for immorality, incompetency, or neglect of duty. The secretary of the board of examiners may be removed for like causes by the members of the board of examiners selected by the township chairmen, acting jointly with the judge of probate; but no member of such board of school examiners, nor the secretary, shall be removed from office without an opportunity to answer to the charges made against him, and all

Vacancy, how filled.

such charges shall be made in writing. Whenever, by death, resignation, removal, or otherwise, a vacancy shall occur in the board of school examiners of any county, other than in the office of secretary, the judge of probate of such county shall have power to fill such vacancy until the first Tuesday in August after his appointment, at which time an examiner shall be elected to fill the unexpired term by the chairmen of the boards of school inspectors of the several townships in the county. Whenever a vacancy occurs in the office of secretary, it shall be filled in the same manner as is provided for the appointment of secretary, in section two of this chapter, and shall be for the unexpired portion of the term for which the vacating secretary was appointed.[k]

(§137.) SEC. 13. All schools which by special enactment may have a district board authorized to inspect and grant certificates to the teachers employed by the same, shall be exempt from the provisions of this chapter as to the examination and licensing of teachers. The officers of every school district which is or shall hereafter be organized in whole or in part in any incorporated city in this State, where no special enactments shall exist in regard to the licensing of teachers, shall have power to examine and license, or cause to be examined and licensed, or may require the county board of examiners to examine and license, teachers for such district, and such license shall be valid not to exceed three years. All city schools having a superintendent employed by their respective boards of education, shall be exempt from the provisions of this chapter, as to the examination and licensing of teachers, and as to the supervision of schools. But all such schools shall, through their proper officers, make such reports as the superintendent of public instruction shall direct.[k]

[k] As amended by Act No. 266, Public Acts of 1887.

CHAPTER XIII.

PENALTIES AND LIABILITIES.

(§138.) SECTION 1. Any taxable inhabitant of a newly formed district receiving the notice of the first meeting, who shall neglect or refuse duly to serve and return such notice, and every chairman of the first district meeting in any district, who shall willfully neglect or refuse to perform the duties enjoined on him in this act shall respectively forfeit the sum of five dollars. *Penalty on inhabitant for neglect of duty.*

(§139.) SEC. 2. Any person duly elected to the office of moderator, director, assessor, or trustee of a school district, who shall neglect or refuse, without sufficient cause, to accept such office and serve therein, or who, having entered upon the duties of his office, shall neglect or refuse to perform any duty required of him by virtue of his office, shall forfeit the sum of ten dollars. *Penalty on district officer for neglecting or refusing to perform duties.*

(§140.) SEC. 3. Any person duly elected or appointed a school inspector, who shall neglect or refuse, without sufficient cause, to qualify and serve as such, or who, having entered upon the duties of his office, shall neglect or refuse to perform any duty required of him by virtue of his office, shall forfeit the sum of ten dollars. *Penalty on inspector for neglect or refusal.*

(§141.) SEC. 4. If any board of school inspectors shall neglect or refuse to make and deliver to the township clerk their annual report as required by this act, within the time limited therefor, they shall be liable to pay the full amount of money lost by their failure, with interest thereon, to be recovered by the township treasurer in the name of the township, in an action of debt, or on the case; and if any township clerk shall neglect or refuse to transmit the report herein mentioned within the time limited therefor, he shall be liable to pay the full amount lost by such neglect or refusal, with interest thereon, to be recovered in an action of debt, or on the case. *Liability of inspectors for neglecting to report.* *Liability of township clerk.*

(§142.) SEC. 5. Any county clerk who shall neglect or refuse to transmit to the superintendent of public instruction the reports required by this act, within the time therefor limited, shall be liable to pay to each township the full amount which such township, or any school district therein, shall lose by such neglect or refusal, with interest thereon, to be recovered in an action of debt, or on the case. *Liability of county clerk for neglect to transmit reports.*

(§143.) SEC. 6. All the moneys collected or received by any township treasurer under the provisions of either of the two last preceding sections, shall be apportioned and distributed to the school districts entitled thereto, in the same manner and in the same proportion that the moneys lost by any neglect or refusal therein mentioned would, according to the provisions of this act, have been apportioned and distributed. *How moneys collected on account of neglect disposed of.*

(§144.) SEC. 7. Any township clerk who shall neglect or refuse to certify to the supervisor any school district taxes that have been reported to him as required by this act, and any supervisor *Liability of township clerk and supervisor in regard to district taxes.*

willfully neglecting to assess any such tax shall be liable to any
district for any damage occasioned thereby, to be recovered by
the assessor in the name of the district, in an action of debt, or
on the case.

When township
board to remove
certain officers.

(§145.) SEC. 8. The township board of each township, and in
the case of fractional school districts, the township board of the
township in which the district school-house thereof is situated,

See App. A.,
¶¶ 12, 17.

shall have power and is hereby required to remove from office,
upon satisfactory proof, after at least five days' notice to the party
implicated, any district officer or school inspector who shall have
illegally used or disposed of any of the public moneys entrusted
to his charge, or who shall persistently and without sufficient
cause refuse or neglect to discharge any of the duties of his office.

Township clerk
to record order
for removal.

And in case of such removal it shall be the duty of the township
clerk of such towship to enter in the records of such township
the resolution or order of such board, for such removal; and such
record of such resolution or order so entered, or a certified copy
thereof, shall br *prima facie* evidence in all courts and places of
the jurisdiction of such board and of the regularity of the proceed-

Party removed
may institute
proceedings for
removal of
order of town-
ship board.

ings for such removal, and (unless the party so removed shall,
within thirty days after such removal, institute proceedings before
a court of competent jurisdiction for the removal of such order
for removal, or if after such thirty days such proceedings to
obtain such removal shall be discontinued or dismissed) shall be
conclusive evidence of jurisdiction and regularity, if it shall
appear that the party so removed had five days' notice of the time
and place fixed by said board for the hearing of the case as
aforesaid.

School officers
and teachers not
to act as school
book agents,
etc.

(§146.) SEC. 9. No school officer, superintendent, or teacher of
schools, shall act as agent for any author, publisher, or seller of
school books, or shall directly or indirectly receive any gift or
reward for his influence in recommending the purchase or use of

School officers
not to be inter-
ested in con-
tracts in cer-
tain cases.

any library or school book or school apparatus, or furniture whatever, nor shall any school officer be personally interested in any
way whatever in any contract with the district in which he may

Such acts
deemed mis-
demeanors.

hold office. Any act or neglect herein prohibited, performed by
any such officer, superintendent, or teacher, shall be deemed a
misdemeanor.

Where this act
shall apply.

(§147.) SEC. 10. All provisions of this act shall apply and be in
force in every school district, township, city and village in this
State, except such as may be inconsistent with the direct provisions of some special enactment of the Legislature.

Chapters and
acts repealed.

(§148.) SEC. 11. Chapters numbered one hundred and thirty-one,
one hundred and thirty-six, one hundred and thirty-seven, and
one hundred and thirty-eight of the compiled laws of eighteen
hundred and seventy-one, and act numbered forty-two of the
session laws of eighteen hundred and seventy-five, and all acts
and parts of acts amendatory of said chapters and said act, being
acts numbered forty-one, forty-two, fifty-six, and sixty-three, of
the session laws of eighteen hundred and seventy-two, acts numbered forty-four, sixty-nine, seventy-one, seventy-six, ninety-

eight, one hundred and nineteen, one hundred and thirty-two, one hundred and sixty-four, and one hundred and ninety-three of the session laws of eighteen hundred and seventy-three, acts numbered thirty-six, fifty-one, eighty-four, ninety-four, one hundred and six, one hundred and thirty-seven, one hundred and eighty-three, and two hundred and thirty of the session laws of eighteen hundred and seventy-five, acts numbered seventy-seven and one hundred and seventy-three of the session laws of eighteen hundred and seventy-seven, acts numbered forty-four, forty-six, one hundred and fifty-nine, one hundred and sixty-four, two hundred and fifty-four, two hundred and fifty-five and two hundred and sixty-four of the session laws of eighteen hundred and seventy-nine, and all other acts and parts of acts contravening the provisions of this act are hereby fully repealed.

CHAPTER XIV.

Act No. 168, Laws of 1881.

ELECTION OF SCHOOL INSPECTORS.

(§149.) SECTION 1. *The People of the State of Michigan enact,* That sections eight and fourteen of chapter twelve, of the compiled laws of eighteen hundred and seventy-one, as amended by act number forty-two of the session laws of eighteen hundred and seventy-five, are hereby amended, and section thirteen of the same chapter, repealed by said act, is hereby restored and amended, and section one hundred and three of the same chapter, as amended by act number one hundred and ninety-nine of the session laws of eighteen hundred and seventy-nine, is hereby amended, all of said sections to read as follows: Sections amended.

(§150.) SEC. 2. The annual meeting of each township shall be held on the first Monday in April, in each year, and at such meeting there shall be an election for the following officers: one supervisor, one township clerk, one treasurer, one school inspector, one commissioner of highways, so many justices of the peace as there are by law to be elected in the township, and so many constables as shall be ordered by the meeting, not exceeding four in number. Annual meeting.
Officers to be elected.

(§151.) SEC. 3. Each school inspector elected as aforesaid shall hold his office for two years from that time and until his successor shall be elected and duly qualified, except when elected or appointed to fill a vacancy, in which case he shall hold the office during the unexpired portion of the regular term: *Provided,* That in the year eighteen hundred and eighty-two one additional school inspector in each township shall be elected for the term of one year: *Provided, further,* That the township superintendent of schools and school inspectors now in office shall continue to act as school inspectors, and said superintendent of schools shall continue to act as chairman of the board of school inspectors until Term of office of school inspectors.
Vacancy.
Proviso.
Proviso.

7

the school inspectors provided for by this act shall have been elected and duly qualified and shall enter upon the duties of their respective offices.

Term of office. (§152.) SEC. 4. Each of the officers elected at such meetings, except justices of the peace and school inspectors, shall hold his office for the term of one year, and until his successor shall be elected and duly qualified.

Who eligible to office. (§153.) SEC. 5. No person, except an elector, as aforesaid, shall be eligible to any elective office contemplated in this chapter:

Proviso. *Provided, however,* That any female person of or above the age of twenty-one years, who has resided in this State three months and in the township ten days next preceding any election, shall be eligible to the office of school inspector.

CHAPTER XV.

Act No. 53, Laws of 1877.

TEACHERS' INSTITUTES.

Examining officers to collect fees from teachers. (§154.) SECTION 1. *The People of the State of Michigan enact,* That all boards or officers authorized by law to examine applicants for certificates of qualification as teachers shall collect, at the time of examination, from each male applicant for a certificate, an annual fee of one dollar, and from each female applicant for a certificate, an annual fee of fifty cents, and the director or secretary of any school board that shall employ any teacher who has not paid the fee hereinbefore provided, shall collect, at the time of making contract, from each male teacher so employed, an annual fee of one dollar, and from each female teacher so employed, an annual fee of fifty cents. All persons paying a fee, as required by this section, shall be given a receipt for the same, and no person shall be required to pay said fee more than once in any school year.[1]

Fees to be paid to county treasurer quarterly. (§155.) SEC. 2. All such fees collected by the director or secretary of any school board shall be paid over to the secretary of the county board of school examiners of the county in which they were collected, on or before the fifteenth day of March, June, September and December, accompanied by a list of those persons from whom they were collected, and all of such fees, together with all those that shall be collected by the county board of school examiners, shall be paid over by the secretary of said board of school examiners to the treasurer of the county in which they were collected, on or before the last day of March, June, September and December, in each year, accompanied by a complete list of all persons from whom said fees were collected; and a like list, accompanied by a statement from the county treasurer

(§154.) The requirement of the statute applies to all teachers, whether applicants for certificates, or employed by school boards, save that but one fee can be required for any one year.—*VanRiper, Attorney General, March 21, 1884.*

[1] As amended by Act No. 112, Session Laws 1883.

that said fees have been paid to him, shall be sent by said secretary to the superintendent of public instruction. All moneys paid over to the county treasurer as provided by this act shall be set apart as a teachers' institute fund, to be used as hereinafter provided.[m] *Fees so paid to constitute teachers' institute fund.*

(§156.) SEC. 3. The superintendent of public instruction shall annually appoint a time and place in each organized county for holding a teachers' institute, make suitable arrangements therefor, and give due notice thereof: *Provided,* That in organized counties having less than one thousand children between the ages of five and twenty years, the holding of said institute shall be optional with the said superintendent, unless requested to hold such institute by fifteen teachers of the county in which such institute is to be held: *Provided, however,* That if there shall not be a sufficient number of teachers in any county to make such request, then teachers of adjoining counties who desire to attend such institute may unite in the required application to said superintendent: *Provided, also,* That the said superintendent may, in his discretion, hold an institute for the benefit of two or more adjoining counties, and draw the institute fund from each of the counties thus benefited, as hereinafter provided.[1] *Annual county institute. Proviso. Proviso. Proviso.*

(§157.) SEC. 4. The superintendent of public instruction, in case of inability personally to conduct any institute or to make the necessary arrangements for holding the same, is hereby authorized to appoint some suitable person for that purpose, who shall be subject to the direction of said superintendent. Every teacher attending any institute held in accordance with the provisions of this act, shall be given by the superintendent of public instruction, or by the duly appointed conductor, a certificate setting forth at what sessions of said institute such teacher shall have been in attendance, and any teacher who shall have closed his or her school in order to attend said institute shall not forfeit his or her wages as teacher during such time as he or she shall have been in attendance at said institute, and the certificate hereinbefore provided shall be evidence of such attendance.[n] *Conductor of institute may be appointed. Teachers can close school to attend institute.*

(§158.) SEC. 5. For the purpose of defraying the expenses of rooms, fires, lights or other necessary charges, and for procuring teachers and lecturers, the said superintendent, or the person duly authorized by him to conduct said institute, may demand of the county clerk of each county for the benefit of which the institute is held, who shall thereupon draw an order on the county treasurer of his county for such sum, not exceeding the amount of the institute fund in the county treasury, as may be necessary to defray the expenses of said institute; and the treasurer of said county is hereby required to pay over to said superintendent or duly appointed institute conductor, from the institute fund in his hands, the amount of said order.[1] *Expenses of institute, how paid.*

[m] As amended by Act No. 112, Session Laws 1883.
[1] As amended by Act No. 68, Laws of 1879.
[n] As amended by Act No. 112, Session Laws of 1883.

May draw on State treasurer, in certain cases.

(§159.) Sec. 6. In case the institute fund in any county shall be insufficient to defray the necessary expenses of any institute held under the provisions of this act, the auditor general shall, upon the certificate of the superintendent that he has made arrangements for holding such institute, and that the county institute fund is insufficient to meet the expenses thereof, draw his warrant upon the state treasurer for such additional sum as said superintendent shall deem necessary for conducting such institute; which sum shall not exceed sixty dollars for each institute of five days' duration, and shall be paid out of the general fund.

Yearly State institute.

Expenses to be paid from State treasury.

(§160.) Sec. 7. The superintendent is authorized to hold, once in each year, an institute for the State at large, to be denominated a State institute; and for the purpose of defraying the necessary expenses of such institute, the auditor general shall, on the certificate of said superintendent that he has made arrangements for holding such institute, draw his warrant upon the state treasurer for such sum as said superintendent shall deem necessary for conducting such institute, which sum shall not exceed four

Proviso.

hundred dollars, and shall be paid out of the general fund: *Provided*, That not more than eighteen hundred dollars shall be drawn from the treasury, or any greater liability incurred in any one year, to meet the provisions of this act.

Vouchers for payments.

(§161.) Sec. 8. The superintendent of public instruction, or the conductor of the institute by him appointed, drawing money from the county treasurer, under section five of this act, shall, at the close of each institute, furnish to the county treasurer, vouchers for all payments from the same in accordance with this act, and he shall return to the county treasurer, whatever of the amount that may remain unexpended, to be replaced in the institute fund.

Acts repealed.

(§162.) Sec. 9. An act entitled " An act to establish teachers' institutes," approved February tenth, eighteen hundred and fifty-five, as amended by act two hundred and thirty-nine, session laws of eighteen hundred and sixty-one, being compiler's sections three thousand seven hundred and eighty-nine, three thousand seven hundred and ninety, and three thousand seven hundred and ninety-one of the compiled laws of eighteen hundred and seventy-one, are hereby repealed.

CHAPTER XVI.

From Act No. 194, Laws of 1889.

NORMAL SCHOOL DIPLOMAS AND CERTIFICATES.

Of the normal school.

(§163.) Section 3. The State board of education shall continue the normal school at Ypsilanti in the county of Washtenaw, where it is now located. The purpose of the normal school shall be the instruction of persons in the art of teaching, and in all the various branches pertaining to the public schools of the State

Proviso.

of Michigan: *Provided*, There shall be prescribed for said school a course of study intended specially to prepare students for the rural and the elementary [graded] schools of this State, which shall provide not less than twenty weeks of special professional instruction.

(§164.) SEC. 5. Said board shall provide all necessary courses of study to be pursued in the normal school and establish and maintain in connection therewith a fully equipped training school as a school of observation and practice, and shall grant, upon the completion of either of said courses, such diplomas as it may deem best, and such diploma, when granted, shall carry with it such honors as the extent of the course for which the diploma is given may warrant and said board of education may direct. Course of study, training school, etc. Diplomas.

(§165.) SEC. 6. Upon the completion of the course specially prescribed, as hereinbefore provided for the rural and elementary graded schools, said board of education shall upon the recommendation of the principal and a majority of the heads of the departments of said school, grant a certificate which shall be signed by said board and the principal of the normal school, which certificate shall contain a list of the studies included in said course, and which shall entitle the holder to teach in any of the schools of the State for which said course has been provided for a period of five years: *Provided*, That said certificate may be suspended or revoked by said State board of education upon cause shown by any county board of examination, or by any board of school officers. Certificate to teach, when granted, term of, etc. Proviso.

(§166.) SEC. 7. Upon the completion of either of the advanced courses of study prescribed by said State board, which shall require not less than four years for their completion, said board of education, upon the recommendation of the principal and a majority of the heads of departments of said school, shall issue a certificate to the person completing said course, which certificate shall be referred to in the diploma hereinbefore provided to be granted. Said certificate shall set forth a list of the studies of the course completed and, when given, shall operate as a life certificate, unless revoked by said State board of education. Life certificates, when granted, etc. May be revoked.

(§167.) SEC. 8. The board of education shall make such regulations for the admission of pupils to said school as it shall deem necessary and proper: *Provided*, That the applicant shall, before admission, sign a declaration of intention to teach in the schools in this State. Admission of pupils. Proviso.

CHAPTER XVII.

From Act No. 194, Laws of 1889.

STATE CERTIFICATES TO TEACHERS.

(§168.) SEC. 15. Said board shall hold at least two meetings each year, at which they shall examine teachers, and grant certificates to such as have taught in the schools of the State at least two years and who shall, upon a thorough and critical examination in every study required for such certificate, be found Board to grant certificates, etc.

to possess eminent scholarship, ability, and good moral character. Such certificate shall be signed by the members of said board and be impressed with its seal and shall entitle the holder to teach in any of the public schools of this State without further examination, and shall be valid for life unless revoked by said board. No certificate shall be granted except upon the examination

Proviso. herein prescribed: *Provided,* That graduates of the literary and scientific departments of the university and of incorporated colleges of the State, shall not be required to teach as a preliminary to taking such examination and certificate.

CHAPTER XVIII.

Act No. 117, Laws of 1855.

TEACHERS' ASSOCIATIONS.

Fifteen or more teachers may form corporation.

(§169.) SECTION 1. *The People of the State of Michigan enact,* Any fifteen or more teachers, or other persons residing in this State, who shall associate for the purpose of promoting education and science, and improvements in the theory and practice of teaching, may form themselves into a corporation, under such

Notice to be published.

name as they may choose, providing they shall have published, in some newspaper printed at Lansing, or in the county in which such association is to be located, for at least one month previous, a notice of the time, place, and purpose of the meeting for such

Constitution, where filed.

association, and shall file in the office of the Secretary of State a copy of the constitution and by-laws of said association.

May hold property.

Restrictions upon its use.

(§170.) SEC. 2 Such association may hold and possess real and personal property to the amount of five thousand dollars; but the funds or property thereof shall not be used for any other purpose than the legitimate business of the association in securing the objects of its corporation.

Privileges and liabilities of corporations.

(§171.) SEC. 3. Upon becoming a corporation, as hereinbefore provided, they shall have all the powers and privileges, and be subject to all the duties of a corporation, according to the provisions of chapter fifty-five of the Revised Statutes of this State [Chap. 130, Compiled Laws of 1871], so far as such provisions shall be applicable in such case, and not inconsistent with the provisions of this act.

CHAPTER XIX.

Act No. 131, Laws of 1875.

SAFE KEEPING OF PUBLIC MONEYS.

"Public moneys" defined.

(§172.) SECTION 1. *The People of the State of Michigan enact,* That all moneys which shall come into the hands of any officer of the State, or of any officer of any county, or of any township, school district, highway district, city or village, or of any other municipal or public corporation within this State, pursuant to any provision of law authorizing such officer to receive the same, shall be denominated public moneys within the meaning of this act.

(§173.) SEC. 2. It shall be the duty of every officer charged with the receiving, keeping, or disbursing of public moneys to keep the same separate and apart from his own money, and he shall not commingle the same with his own money, nor with the money of any other person, firm, or corporation. *Public moneys to be kept separate from all other funds.*

(§174.) SEC. 3. No such officer shall, under any pretext, use nor allow to be used, any such moneys for any purpose other than in accordance with the provisions of law; nor shall he .use the same for his own private use, nor loan the same to any person, firm, or corporation without legal authority so to do. *How used.*

(§175.) SEC. 4. In all cases where public moneys are authorized to be deposited in any bank, or to be loaned to any individual, firm or corporation, for interest, the interest accruing upon such public moneys shall belong to and constitute a general fund of the State, county, or other public or municipal corporation, as the case may be. *Interest on public moneys to constitute a general fund.*

(§176.) SEC. 5. In no case shall any such officer, directly or indirectly, receive any pecuniary or valuable consideration as an inducement for the deposit of any public moneys with any particular bank, person, firm or corporation. *Officers not to receive consideration for deposit of money with particular bank, etc.*

(§177.) SEC. 6. The provisions of this act shall apply to all deputies of such officer or officers, and to all clerks, agents, and servants of such officer or officers. *Provisions of this act to apply to deputies, etc.*

(§178.) SEC. 7. Any person guilty of a violation of any of the provisions of this act shall, on conviction thereof, be punished by a fine not exceeding one thousand dollars, or imprisonment in the county jail not exceeding six months, or both such fine and imprisonment in the discretion of the court: *Provided,* That nothing in this act contained shall prevent a prosecution under the general statute for embezzlement in cases where the facts warrant a prosecution under such general statute. *Penalty for violating provisions of this act. Proviso.*

(§179.) SEC. 8. Any officer who shall willfully or corruptly draw or issue any warrant, order, or certificate for the payment of money in excess of the amount authorized by law, or for a purpose not authorized by law, shall be deemed guilty of a misdemeanor, and may be punished as provided in the preceding section. *Penalty for illegal payment of money.*

CHAPTER XX.*

Act No. 144, Laws of 1883, as amended by Act No. 108, Laws of 1885.

COMPULSORY EDUCATION OF CHILDREN.

(§180.) SECTION 1. *The People of the State of Michigan enact,* That every parent, guardian, or other person in [the State of *Duty of parents and guardians to send children to school.*

* Act No. 144, Session Laws of 1883, consisted of thirteen sections. Act No. 108, Session Laws of 1885, repealed sections six, seven, eight, nine, ten, and eleven, leaving but seven sections in force. Sections six and seven of the above chapter are numbered twelve and thirteen in the Act as passed at the legislative session of 1883. (See Chapter XXI of this volume.)

Michigan, having control and charge of any child or children between the ages of eight and .fourteen years, shall be required to send such child or children to a public school for a period of at least four months in each school year, commencing on the first Monday of September in the year eighteen hundred and eighty-three, at least six weeks of which shall be consecutive, unless such child or children are excused from such attendance by the board of the school district in which such parents or guardians reside, upon its being shown to their satisfaction that his bodily or mental condition has been such as to prevent his attendance at school, or application to study for the period required, or that such child or children are taught in a private school, or at home, in such branches as are usually taught in primary schools, or have already acquired the ordinary branches of learning taught in public schools: *Provided*, In case a public school shall not be taught for four months during the year within two miles, by the nearest traveled road, of the residence of any person within the school district, he shall not be liable to the provisions of this act.

Proviso.

Children cannot be employed to labor in certain cases. (§181.) SEC. 2. No child under the age of fourteen years shall be employed by any person, company or corporation, to labor in any business, unless such child shall have attended some public or private day school where instruction was given by a teacher qualified to instruct in such branches as are usually taught in primary schools, at least four months of the twelve months next preceding the month in which such child shall be so employed: *Provided,* That a certificate from the director of the school district in which such child shall have attended school shall be evidence of a compliance with the provisions of this act.[*]

Proviso.

Children unemployed to attend school. (§182.) SEC. 3. Every parent, guardian, or other person, having charge or control of any child from eight to fourteen years of age, who has been temporarily discharged from any business or employment, shall send such child to some public or private day school for the period for which such child shall have been discharged, unless such child shall have been excused from such attendance by the board of the school district, for reasons as stated in section one hereof.

District board to furnish text-books. (§183.) SEC. 4. It shall be the duty of the school district board of each district of the State to purchase and furnish, at the expense of the district, such text-books as may in the judgment of said board be necessary for the use of children whose parents are not able to furnish the same, the expense of such books to be levied in like manner as other district taxes.

Penalty for non-compliance with foregoing sections. (§184.) SEC. 5. In case any parent, guardian, or other person shall fail to comply with the provisions of sections two, three, or four of this act, such parent, guardian, or other person shall be deemed guilty of a misdemeanor, and shall, on conviction, be liable to a fine of not less than five dollars nor more than ten dollars for the first offense, and of not less than ten dollars for ach subsequent offense.[*]

[*] See Chapter XXII of this volume.

(§185.) SEC. 6. It shall be the duty of the officers detailed or appointed under the provisions of this act to assist in the enforcement thereof, to institute, or cause to be instituted, proceedings against any parent, guardian, or other person having legal charge and control of any child, or any person, company, or corporation, violating any of the provisions of sections one, two, three, four, and five of this act; and in school districts and cities, and villages of less than five thousand inhabitants, it shall be the duty of the school board to institute, or cause to be instituted, such proceedings.* <small>Truant officers empowered to institute proceedings.</small>

(§186.) SEC. 7. When any of the provisions of this act are violated by a corporation, proceedings may be had against any of the officers or agents of said corporation, who in any way participate in or are cognizant of such violation by the corporation of which they are the officers or agents, and said officers or agents shall be subject to the same penalties as individuals similarly offending.* <small>Proceedings may be had against officers of corporations.</small>

CHAPTER XXI.

Act No. 108, Laws of 1885, as amended by Act No. 218, Public Acts of 1889.

COMPULSORY REFORMATORY EDUCATION OF JUVENILE DISORDERLY PERSONS.

(§187.) SECTION 1. In all cities, villages and townships in this State maintaining and supporting a graded school, the board of education, school board or other officer or officers having charge of the schools of said cities, villages and townships may establish one or more ungraded schools for the instruction of certain children, as defined and set forth in the following sections, and they may, through their authorized agents or officers, require said children to attend said ungraded schools or any department of their graded schools, as said [board] of education or school board may designate, during the whole or a portion of each school day, as they may direct. <small>Ungraded schools may be established in certain municipalities.</small> <small>Attendance on ungraded school required.</small>

(§188.) SEC. 2. In all cities having a duly organized police force, it shall be the duty of the police authority, at the request of the school authority, to detail one or more members of said force to assist in the enforcement of this act; and in cities, villages, or townships having no regular police force, it shall be the duty of the board of education, or the school district officers, to designate the marshal of such city, or village, or one or more constables of said city, village or township, whose duty it shall be to assist in the enforcement of this act, as occasion may require, and board of education or school board shall fix and determine the compensation to be paid such officer for the performance of his duties under this act, and shall pay the same <small>Appointment of truant officers.</small> <small>Compensation fixed by board of education.</small>

---

* Act No. 141, Session Laws of 1883, consisted of thirteen sections. Act No. 108, Session Laws of 1885, repealed sections six, seven, eight, nine, ten, and eleven, leaving but seven sections in force. Sections six and seven of the above chapter are numbered twelve and thirteen in the Act as passed at the legislative session of 1883. (See Chapter XXI of this volume.)

from any moneys in their hands raised or provided for the general expenses of the public schools. Members of any police force, marshal, or constable designated to assist in the enforcement of this act, as provided in this section, shall be known as truant officers.

Who shall be deemed juvenile disorderly persons. (§189.) SEC. 3. The following classes of persons between the ages of eight and sixteen years shall be deemed juvenile disorderly persons, and shall be subject to the provisions of this act:

Class One, Habitual truants from any school in which they are enrolled as pupils;

Class Two, Children who, while attending any public school, are incorrigibly turbulent, disobedient, or insubordinate, or are vicious or immoral in conduct;

Class Three, Children who are not attending any school, and who habitually frequent streets and other public places, having no lawful business, employment, or occupation, which renders attendance at school impossible.

Truant officers to notify truants, etc. (§190.) SEC. 4. It shall be the duty of the truant officers, under the direction of the aforesaid school authorities, or their authorized agents, to warn alleged truants and incorrigibles, and their parents or guardians, of the consequences of belonging to any of said classes of juvenile disorderly persons, as set forth and defined in this act. They shall also, under direction as aforesaid, serve written or printed notice upon the parent or guardian of any child belonging to class one, or to class two, as described and defined in section three of this act, that such child must begin regular attendance at such school within five days of the date of service of such notice.

Truant officer to notify parent, etc. (§191.) SEC. 5. They shall also under direction, as aforesaid, give written or printed notice to the parent or guardian of any child belonging to class three, as described and defined in section three of this act, that said child is not attending any school and require said parent or guardian to cause said child to begin regular attendance at such school within five days of the date of the service of said notice.

Truant officer to make complaint in certain cases. (§192.) SEC. 6. If said parent or guardian, or other person having the legal charge and control of said child shall willfully refuse, fail, or neglect to cause said child to attend such school, after notice given, as prescribed in sections four and five of this act, it shall be the duty of said officer to make or cause to be made a complaint against said parent, guardian, or other person **What courts shall have jurisdiction.** having the legal charge and control of such child, before a justice of the peace in the city, village or township where the party resides, except in cities having a recorder's or police court, when complaint shall be made in said recorder's or police court, for such refusal or neglect, and said justice of the peace, police judge, or recorder's court shall issue a warrant upon said complaint and shall proceed to hear and determine the same, and upon conviction thereof said parent, guardian, or other person, as the case may be, shall be punished by a fine not less than ten

*See Chapter XXII of this volume.

dollars, nor more than twenty-five dollars, or the court may in its discretion, require the person so convicted to give a bond in the penal sum of one hundred dollars with one or more sureties to be approved by said court, conditioned that said person so convicted shall cause the child or children under his legal charge or control, to attend at such school within five days thereafter, and to remain at said school during a full school term of twenty school weeks, dating from time of beginning of said attendance: *Provided*, That if said parent or guardian, or other person in charge of said child shall under oath plead inability to cause said child to attend said school, then said parent or guardian or other person shall be discharged, and said justice of the peace, or court shall, upon complaint of said truant officer, or other person that said child is a juvenile disorderly person, as described in section three of this act, issue a warrant and proceed to hear such complaint, and if said justice of the peace or court shall determine that said child is a juvenile disorderly person within the meaning of this act, then said justice of the peace or court shall thereupon, and after consultation with the county agent, sentence said child, if a boy, to the reform school at Lansing, or if a girl, to the industrial home for girls at Adrian, as the case may be, for one year or for a longer term, not extending beyond the time when said child shall arrive at the age of sixteen years, unless sooner discharged by the board of control of said reform school, or industrial home for girls: *Provided however*, That such sentence may be suspended in the discretion of the said justice of the peace, police judge, or judge of the recorder's court, for such time as said child shall regularly attend school, and properly deport himself or herself: *It is further provided*, That if for any cause the parent or guardian, or other person having charge of any juvenile disorderly person, as defined in this act, shall fail, after notice as heretofore prescribed in this act, to cause such juvenile disorderly person to attend said school, or if such parent, guardian, or other person shall make the complaint as provided in this act without proceedings having been taken against him as in this act provided, or if said juvenile disorderly person have no parent or guardian then complaint against such juvenile disorderly person may be made, heard, tried, and determined in the same manner as is provided for in case the parent pleads inability to cause said juvenile disorderly person to attend said school: *And it is further provided*, That no child under the age of ten years shall be sent to the reform school, or industrial home for girls.

(§193.) SEC. 7. When it appears to the school authorities that the parent, guardian, or other person is unable to provide suitable books for said child, said child shall be furnished by the school board with such books as are required in the course of studies pursued in such school, and said books shall be the same in all respects as those in use in other schools in said city, village, or township and no distinction in form, color, labeling, or substance shall be permitted. The expense of said books shall be paid for

[Marginal notes:] Penalty imposed. — When parent, etc., shall be discharged. — Juvenile disorderly person to be sentenced to reform school or industrial home for girls. — Court may suspend sentence in certain cases. — Children under ten years not to be sentenced. — School board to provide text-books for certain children.

from the school fund of said municipality and levied and collected in the same manner as all other school taxes.

Certain existing legal provisions not applicable to class of persons provided for in this act.

(§194) SEC. 8. It is further provided that the provisions of act number one hundred and forty-four of the public acts of eighteen hundred and eighty-three, entitled "An act to provide for the compulsory education of children in certain cases," approved May thirty-first, eighteen hundred and eighty-three, limiting such compulsory education to a period not exceeding four months in any one year shall not, so far as said limitation is concerned,

Certain sections repealed.

have any application to the class of juvenile disorderly persons provided for in this act. It is also provided that sections six, seven, eight, nine, ten, and eleven, of act one hundred and forty-four, of the session laws of eighteen hundred and eighty-three, and all acts and parts of acts inconsistent with the provisions of this act are hereby repealed.

CHAPTER XXII.

Act No. 39, Laws of 1885, as amended by Act No. 21, Public Acts of 1889.

REGULATING THE EMPLOYMENT OF CHILDREN.

Children under ten years.

(§195.) SECTION 1. *The People of the State of Michigan enact,* That no child under the age of ten years shall be employed in any factory, warehouse or workshop where the manufacture of any goods whatever is carried on, or where any goods are prepared for manufacturing.

Children not to be employed in certain cases.

(§196.) SEC. 2. No child under the age of fourteen years shall be employed by any person to labor in any business, unless such child shall have attended some public or private day school, where instruction was given by a teacher qualified to instruct in such branches as are usually taught in primary schools, at least four months of the twelve months next preceding the month in which such child shall be so employed, except in districts in which only

Proviso.

three months of school are taught by a qualified teacher : *Provided*, That a certificate of such attendance from the superintendent of the school, or the director of the school district in which such child shall have so attended school, shall be evidence of a compliance with the provisions of this section, if acted upon by the employer in good faith. If any such superintendent or director shall knowingly make a false certificate, he shall be deemed guilty of a violation of this act, and shall be liable to the punishment hereinafter provided.

Certificate of attendance at school to be filed by employer.

(§197.) SEC. 3. Certificates given under the preceding section shall be deposited with the employer, at the time of employing any such child, and shall be kept by him on file in his office, and shall, at all times, be subject to inspection by the persons authorized to make inspections under this act.

Under 18 years limitation 10 hours.

(§198.) SEC. 4. No child, or young person under the age, of eighteen years, and no woman, shall be employed in any factory, warehouse, workshop or place where the manufacture of any kind of goods is carried on, or where any goods are prepared for manufacturing, for a longer period than an average of ten hours in a day, or sixty hours in any week, and at least one hour shall be allowed in the labor period of each day for dinner. *Dinner hour.*

(§199.) SEC. 5. Every person who shall employ any female in any factory, warehouse, workshop, store or hotel shall provide suitable seats for the use of the females so employed, and shall permit the use of such seats by them when they are not necessarily engaged in the active duties for which they are employed. *Seats for female employes.*

(§200.) SEC. 6. Any person, company or corporation who shall violate any of the provisions of this act, shall, for each offense, forfeit a penalty of fifty dollars, to be recovered before any competent court. *Penalty for violating provisions of this act.*

(§201.) SEC. 7. In all cities it shall be the duty of the superintendent, or chief officer of police, by suitable inspections, to see that the regulations of this act are observed, and also to prosecute all persons who shall violate the same. Such superintendent, or chief officer of police, shall detail such portion of the force under him as he shall deem necessary, for the inspection, from time to time, of all the aforesaid places where such children or young persons may be employed: *Provided,* That, in the city of Detroit, the board of building inspectors of said city, or any member thereof, shall have concurrent jurisdiction with the superintendent or chief officer of police with like power and authority to personally see that the regulations of this act are observed and also to enter complaint against all persons who shall violate the same. In towns the supervisors thereof shall perform the duties above imposed on the superintendent, or chief officer of police in cities. *Duty of officers to make inspection. Proviso for city of Detroit.*

(§202) SEC. 8. The directors of any corporation which shall willfully neglect or refuse to obey the provisions of this act, shall each be liable to the penalties of this act: *Provided,* That the provisions of this act shall not apply to any of the penal, reformatory, or benevolent institutions of this State. *Directors of corporation personally liable.*

CHAPTER XXIII.

Act No. 222, Public Acts of 1887.

TO PREVENT CRIME AND PUNISH TRUANCY.

(§203.) SECTION 1. *The People of the State of Michigan enact,* That any girl between the ages of ten and seventeen years, or boy between the ages of ten and sixteen years, who shall run away, or wilfully absent himself or herself from the school he or she is attending, or from any house, office, shop, farm or other place where such person is legitimately employed to labor, or shall frequent saloons or other places where intoxicating liquors are kept for sale, or shall be found lounging around the same, or shall be found lounging upon the public streets, or other public places of any city or village, against the command of his or her parent or guardian, or shall, without the permission of his or her parents *Certain girls and boys deemed truant and disorderly persons.*

or guardian, attend any public dance, skating rink or show, shall be deemed to be a truant and disorderly person.

Who to make complaint.

(§204.) SEC. 2. Upon complaint upon oath and in writing made before any justice of the peace by the parent or guardian of any girl between the ages of ten and seventeen years, or of any boy between ten and sixteen years of age, or by the supervisor of any township, or the mayor of any city, or president of any village, and in cities of over eight thousand population, by the chief of police, that any such minor has been guilty of any of the acts specified in section one of this act, such justice shall issue his

Upon conviction, where to be sentenced.

warrant for the arrest of such minor, and upon such conviction, such minor, if a boy, may be sentenced by such justice to the reform school for boys at Lansing; and if a girl, to the State

Term of sentence.

industrial home for girls at Adrian; boys until seventeen years of age and girls until twenty-one years of age, unless sooner dis-

Proviso as to approval of sentence.

charged according to law: *Provided*, That no person or persons shall be sent to said reform school for boys, or the industrial home for girls until the sentence therein has been submitted to and approved by the circuit judge of the circuit or the judge of probate of the county in which such conviction shall be had.

Proceedings upon trial.

(§205.) SEC. 3. The same proceedings shall be had upon the trial of any person charged with being guilty of any of the offenses mentioned in section one of this act before the justice before whom such person is brought as are had in trials for mis-

Duty of State agent.

demeanor, as far as the same are applicable, and the State agent for the care of juvenile offenders of the county wherein such offenders may be on trial shall have authority and take the same action in the premises as is provided by act number one hundred and seventy-one of the session laws of eighteen hundred and seventy-three of this State.

CHAPTER XXIV.

Act No. 147, Public Acts of 1889.

FREE TEXT BOOKS.

District to vote on question of furnishing free text-books.

(§206.) SECTION 1. *The People of the State of Michigan enact*, That from and after June thirtieth, eighteen hundred and ninety, each school board of the State shall purchase, when authorized, as hereinafter provided, the text books used by the pupils of the schools in its district in each of the following subjects, to wit: Orthography, spelling, writing, reading, geography, arithmetic, grammar (including language lessons), national and State history, civil government, and physiology and hygiene; but text books once adopted under the provisions of this act shall not

Proviso.

be changed within five years: *Provided*, That the text book on the subject of physiology and hygiene must be approved by the State board of education, and shall in every way comply with section fifteen of act number one hundred and sixty-five of the public acts of eighteen hundred and eighty-seven, approved June

ninth, eighteen hundred and eighty-seven : *And provided fur-* Proviso.
ther, That all text books used in any district shall be uniform in
any one subject.

(§207.) SEC. 2. The district board of each school district shall District board to select text-books.
select the kind of text books on subjects enumerated in section
one to be taught in schools of their respective districts : *Provided*,
That nothing herein contained shall require any change in text Vote to be taken at first annual meeting after the passage of this act.
books now in use in such district. They shall cause to be posted
in a conspicuous place, at least ten days prior to the first annual
school meeting from and after the passage of this act, a notice
that those qualified to vote upon the question of raising money
in said district shall vote at such annual meeting to authorize
said district board to purchase and provide free text books for
the use of the pupils in said district. If a majority of all the
voters, as above provided, present at such meeting shall authorize said board to raise by tax a sum sufficient to comply with
the provisions of this act, the district board shall thereupon
make a list of such books and file one copy with the township
clerk and keep one copy posted in the school, and due notice of
such action by the district shall be noted in the annual report to
the superintendent of public instruction. The district board District board to purchase text-books when authorized.
shall take the necessary steps to purchase such books for the use
of all pupils in the several schools of their district, as hereinafter
provided. The text books so purchased shall be the property
of the district purchasing the same, and shall be loaned to pupils
free of charge, under such rules and regulations for their careful
use and return as said district board may establish : *Provided*, Proviso.
That nothing herein contained shall prevent any person from
buying his or her books from the district board of the school in
which he or she may attend : *Provided further*, That nothing Proviso.
herein contained shall prevent any district having once adopted
or rejected free text books from taking further action on the
same at any subsequent annual meeting.

(§208.) SEC. 3. It shall be the duty of the district board of Board to con-tract with pub-lishers, etc.
any school district adopting free text books provided for in this
act to make a contract with some dealer or publisher to furnish
books used in said district at a price not greater than the net
wholesale price of such books : *Provided*, That any district may, Proviso.
if it so desires, authorize its district board to advertise for pro-
posals before making such contract.

(§209.) SEC. 4. The district board of every school district in Board to make annual estimate of amount to be raised.
the State adopting free text books under this act shall make and
prepare annually an estimate of the amount of money necessary
to be raised to comply with the conditions of this act and shall
add such amount to the annual estimates made for money to be
raised for school purposes, for the next ensuing year. Said sum
shall be in addition to the amount now provided by law to be
raised ; which amount each township clerk shall certify to the
supervisor of his township to be assessed upon the taxable property of the respective districts as provided by law for raising the
regular annual estimates of the respective district boards for

school purposes and when collected shall be paid to the district treasurer in the same manner as all other money belonging to said district is paid.

When director to purchase books, etc. (§210.) SEC. 5. On the first day of February next after the tax shall have been levied, the director of said district may proceed to purchase the books required by the pupils of his district from the list mentioned in section one of this act, and shall draw his warrant, countersigned by the moderator, upon the treasurer or assessor of the district for the price of the books so purchased, including the cost of transportation.

Refusal or neglect of duty a misdemeanor. (§211.) SEC. 6. If the officers of any school district, which has so voted to supply itself with text books, shall refuse or neglect to purchase at the expense of the district for the use of the pupils thereof, the text books as enumerated in section one of this act, or to provide the money therefor as herein prescribed, each officer or member of such board so refusing, or neglecting, **Penalty.** shall be deemed guilty of a misdemeanor, and upon conviction thereof before a court of competent jurisdiction, shall be liable to a penalty of not more than fifty dollars or imprisonment in the county jail for a period not exceeding thirty days or by both such **Proviso.** fine and imprisonment in the discretion of the court: *Provided,* That any district board may buy its books of local dealers if the same can be purchased and delivered to the director as cheap as if bought of the party who makes the lowest bid to the district **Further proviso.** board: *Provided further,* That school districts in cities organized under special charters shall be exempt from the provisions of **In cities boards may submit question to voters of district.** this act, but such districts may, when so authorized by a majority vote of their district boards, submit the question of free text books to the qualified voters of said districts. If a majority of the qualified electors vote in favor of furnishing free text books, such district boards shall have authority to proceed under the provisions of this act.

NOTE.

APPORTIONMENT OF SURPLUS DOG-TAX TO SCHOOL DISTRICTS.

Under the provisions of Act No. 198, Public Acts of 1877, as amended by Act No. 283 of the Public Acts of 1881, it is required that in all the townships and cities of the State there shall annually be levied and collected a tax of one dollar upon every male dog and of three dollars upon every female dog. The money thus obtained is to constitute a fund in the several townships and cities for the payment of damages sustained by owners of sheep by reason of having such sheep killed or wounded by dogs. Section six of the law referred to provides that "if money remains of such fund after satisfactory payment of all claims aforesaid in any one year over and above the sum of one hundred.

dollars, it shall be apportioned among the several school districts of such township or city in proportion to the number of children therein of school age." The apportionment must be based upon the whole number of children of school age residing in the township, and include all districts whether lying wholly or partly in such township. In case of a fractional district in which the school-house is situated in a different township, the money belonging to such district must be paid over to the treasurer of the township in which the school-house is situated, and by that treasurer paid to the district, in the same way as in the case of the one-mill and other taxes.

By Act No. 214, Public Acts of 1889, it is provided that if any money remains in this fund in any city and any township or part of township adjoining thereto (the same being within one county) "after the payment of the orders payable out of the same and the amount of said money shall exceed the sum of two hundred dollars, the sum in excess of two hundred dollars shall be apportioned by said county treasurer to the said township or part of township and said city in proportion to the amount contributed to said fund during the preceding year, and the amount so apportioned to any said township or part of township, or said city, shall be respectively apportioned among the several school districts of said township or part of township and said city, in proportion to the number of children therein of school age.''

9

APPENDIX A.

DIGEST OF DECISIONS OF THE SUPREME COURT.

I.

TOWNSHIP BOARD OF SCHOOL INSPECTORS.

¶1. The statutory notice of meetings by inspectors must be given, stating the object of the meeting. And no business at a meeting inconsistent with the notice is lawful. *Passage v. School Inspectors of Williamstown,* 19|Mich., 330.

¶2. The township board of school inspectors have no power to dissolve a school district erected by special act of the legislature, and to set back the territory into the districts from which it was taken. *School District v. Dean,* 17 Mich., 223.

¶3. On the erection and organization of a new township, the inspectors of such township may sever its territory from the school district within which it was formerly embraced, and there is no general provision of law which charges the property within the new township with the obligation to pay any debts created for school purposes, which existed at the time of the erection of the new township. *School District No. 1 of Portage v. Ryan,* 19|Mich., 203.

¶4. *Mandamus* will not be granted to disturb an apportionment made by the township board of school inspectors between different districts, acquiesced in for several years, and which if the court could change it has no proof that it ought to. *School District No. 3 of Riverside Township v. the Township of Riverside,* 67 Mich., 404.

II.

APPEALS FROM ACTION OF SCHOOL INSPECTORS.

¶5. Under the statute providing for appeals from the board of school inspectors to the township board, the approval of the appeal bond is essential to complete an appeal; and the fact that the bond was presented to the clerk of the board of inspectors, who refused to approve it because it was not witnessed, even though the objection be a frivolous one, made in bad faith and for vexation, will not render the bond sufficient without an approval, since, under the statute, it may be approved also by any justice of the township. *Clement v. Everest*, 29 Mich., 19.

¶6. The validity of the action of school inspectors in changing the boundaries of school districts is not affected by the fact that the inspectors were interested parties as taxpayers and residents; the disabling doctrine has no application to those administrative acts which are public, and not with or between private parties. *Ibid.*

¶7. The regularity of the action of school inspectors in creating or changing school districts will not be inquired into in a collateral proceeding; their action is the exercise of a public discretionary power, which can only be reviewed, if at all, by some direct appellate process authorized by law and operating upon the proceedings themselves to affirm, reverse or change them. *Ibid.*

¶8. Parties appealing under the statute from the action of school inspectors in arranging school districts, to the township board, thereby waive those questions which require judicial review and submit themselves to the discretion of that body; and a *certiorari* to the township board does not open for review the doings of the inspectors. *Brody v. Township Board of Penn*, 32 Mich., 272.

¶9. It was never intended that a court should exercise any of these powers of discretionary administration; and when, on such appeal, the township board acted within its jurisdiction, its discretion cannot be reviewed by the courts; and if it did not, and its acts were void, then under the statute the action of the inspectors, after ten days, is equally intact and beyond disturbance. *Ibid.*

¶10. Where, however, the township board, acting without authority, reverses the action of the inspectors, their doings may be overturned; but an order of the board affirming the action of the inspectors, whether properly or improperly, only leaves such action where it would have been without such interference. *Ibid.*

¶11. A township board has jurisdiction of appeals from decisions of the board of school inspectors fixing the amount to be paid by an old school district to a new one where the latter comprises part of the same territory, and the former retains the school property. *School District No. Five of Pine Township v. Wilcox*, 48 Mich., 404.

III.

TOWNSHIP BOARD.

¶12. An application to the township board to remove the moderator of a school district, on the ground that he presistently refuses to countersign an order drawn by the director of the district on the assessor, involves an inquiry, in which the payee named in the order is an interested party. *Stockwell v. Township Board of White Lake*, 22 Mich., 341.

¶13. A proceeding before the township board to remove an officer of a school district, is in the nature of a judicial investigation; and when one of the board is interested in the subject of the complaint, and the presence of such member is essential to the quorum, the proceedings are void. *Ibid.*

¶14. When either of the members of the township board is interested in the subject for consideration, he is not "competent or able to act," in the sense of the statute; and such incompetency will justify the calling in of one of the remaining justices. *Ibid.*

¶15. Every special tribunal appointed by law is subject to the maxim that no person can sit in any cause in which he is a party, or in which he is interested. *Ibid.*

¶16. The removal of a school district assessor by the township board is reviewable on *certiorari*. *Merrick v. Township Board*, 41 Mich., 630.

¶17. Costs awarded by the supreme court in a proceeding by *certiorari* against persons composing a township board, to review their official acts, are to be collected like township charges, and not by execution against the officers personally. *Stockwell v. Township Board of White Lake*, 22 Mich., 341.

¶18. Proceedings by a township board to remove a school director are not invalidated by the fact that it did not meet to agree on the notice under which the proceedings were taken. *Wenzell v. Township Board of Dorr*, 49 Mich., 25.

¶19. The primary school law does not authorize the township board to remove the moderator for hiring her husband to teach the district school and agreeing to pay him more than is necessary to secure a better teacher. *Hazen v. Town Board of Akron*, 48 Mich., 188.

¶20. In providing that the school director shall keep the necessary schoolhouse furniture in due order and condition, and that his expenses shall be subsequently audited and paid, it is not intended that money must be put into his hands beforehand. *Township Board of Hamtramck v. Holihan*, 46 Mich., 127.

¶21. The township board is exclusive judge of the facts on which it is authorized to remove a school director, and its proceedings can only be reviewed by the circuit and supreme courts on questions of law. *Ibid.*

¶22. Proceedings by a township board to remove a school director cannot properly be taken until the action of the proper authorities has been invoked by complaint of some definite violation of duty; but where the plaintiff admits the charges set up against him, and expressly desires the board to act on them without farther delay, he cannot afterwards complain that they did so. *Geddes v. Township of Thomastown*, 46 Mich., 316.

¶23. The action of a town board in removing a school director is final, unless speedily brought up for review. *Ibid.*

¶24. The willful refusal of a school director to sign a contract made with a teacher, or to accept and file it, or draw orders for the teacher's pay while it is pending, and his obstinate neglect to furnish necessary school-house supplies, may be taken into account in proceedings for his removal. *Ibid.*

IV.

ORGANIZATION OF SCHOOL DISTRICTS.

¶25. There should be some special and extraordinary reason to justify interference by *quo warranto* with the organization of a school district, as the statutes provide a speedier remedy by an appeal from the inspectors to the township board. *Lord v. Every*, 38 Mich., 405.

¶26. When a school district had enjoyed its franchises for five years, during most of which time proceedings to inquire into the validity of the organization had been pending by *quo warranto* and writ of error instead of the speedier statutory process of appeal, the supreme court declined to review its organization on technicalities. *Ibid.*

¶27. The legal organization of a school district actually exercising its corporate powers, cannot be collaterally questioned in contesting a title based on a school tax. *Stockle et al. v. Silsbee*, 41 Mich., 615.

¶28. A *certiorari* to review proceedings whereby a new school district has been created out of old districts, must be applied for before the district has been organized and assumed the functions of a corporation; after that time the proper course is to take measures to try the legality of its corporate existence by *quo warranto*, or other direct proceeding against the alleged corporation or its officers. *Fractional School District No. 1 of Owosso, etc., v. School Inspectors of Owosso, etc.*, 27 Mich., 3.

¶29. *Certiorari* addressed to the assessor of a school district is wholly unsuited as a remedy to test the legal organization and existence of the district, as the errors, if any there are, lie back of any action of the assessor, and are to be found in the action of the township authorities. *Jaquith v. Hale*, 31 Mich., 430.

¶30. It has always been the policy of the Michigan school laws that no primary school district should contain more than nine sections of land. *Simpkins et al. v. School District No. 1 of Michigamme et al.*, 45 Mich., 559.

¶31. Township school inspectors cannot enlarge a graded school district by adding unorganized territory, though they may, with the consent of the trustees, transfer to its jurisdiction territory previously organized into primary districts. *Ibid.*

¶32. Injunction lies to restrain the sale, for school taxes, of lands unlawfully included within the taxing district. *Ibid.*

¶33. A writ of *certiorari* to bring up proceedings for the formation of a school district will not be sustained if after its issue, and without good reason, it has been allowed to sleep until the organization has been completed, a tax voted and contract made for building a school-house, and interests established which cannot be overturned without public inconvenience and injury and individual damage. *Parman v. Board of School Inspectors*, 49 Mich., 63.

¶34. Where *certiorari* issues to bring up proceedings for the formation of a school district, the papers on which it was allowed must be served with it. *Ibid.*

¶35. Where there has been actual notice of proposed proceedings by joint boards for the formation of a new school district out of several old ones, mere informalities in the issue of such notice are not jurisdictional defects; nor is the fact that it covers territory not actually taken. *Ibid.*

¶36. The statutory requirement for notice of the meeting of a township board of school inspectors to alter the boundaries of a school district, is jurisdictional, and proof of posting such notice should be filed with the clerk of the board, before any action is taken. *Coulter et al. v. Board of School Inspectors of Grant and Arthur Townships*, 59 Mich., 391.

¶37. In the absence of the consent of the owners of lands which have been taxed for building a school-house, within three years last preceding the date of their proposed transfer to another district, such transfer is illegal; and the fact that the detached territory was not at the same time attached to another district will not legalize such transfer. *Ibid.*

¶38. The statutory requirement for notice of the meeting of a township board of school inspectors to alter the boundaries of a district is jurisdictional, and until such notice has been given, and proof of posting made, as required by law, the inspectors have no power to act. *Fractional School District No. 3 of Martin, Watson and Wayland Townships v. Boards of School Inspectors of said Townships*, 63 Mich., 611.

¶39. Where a *de facto* school district has exercised its franchises and privileges for over *two* years, it is presumed to have been *legally* organized, and it is too late to litigate that question in law or equity. *School District No. 3 of Everett Township v. School District No. 1 of Wilcox Township*, 63 Mich., 51.

¶40. The statutory provision requiring the town clerk to give notice of every meeting of the board of school inspectors of his township, existing prior to the 1881 amendment, was imperative, and the apportionment by the inspectors of the valuation of school property, on the formation of a new district, at a meeting held without such notice, was *void*; and a bill in equity will lie in the name of the old district to enjoin the assessment and collection of a tax to satisfy the amount so apportioned as its share of such valuation. *Ibid.*

¶41. A township board of school inspectors may under *one notice*, and at *one meeting*, by *separate action*, detach lands from *separate* school districts and attach them to one district. *Doxey v. The Township Board of School Inspectors of Martin Township*, 67 Mich., 601.

¶42. Where the action of a board of school inspectors in *detaching* territory from a district, without the consent of a majority of the resident taxpayers, and *attaching* it to another district, left land enough in the former for school purposes, they may afterwards consolidate such remaining territory, with the consent of its remaining tax-payers, with any other district which gives a like consent. *Ibid.*

¶43. At a school meeting to vote on the question of dissolving the district, 18 votes were cast in favor of the proposition, and 9 against it. Every person present who possessed the qualifications of a voter at any school meeting was allowed to vote, without reference to sex, or whether or not he or she was a resident tax-payer. Ten or more persons who were not resident tax-payers voted, and some of the legal tax-payers did not vote, and some were not present. *Held*, that the consent of a majority of the resident tax-payers had not been obtained as required by Howell's Statutes §5041. *Briggs v. Borden et al., School Inspectors*, 38 N. W. Rep., 712.

¶44. A bill will lie, at the suit of resident tax-payer, to restrain the board of school inspectors from selling a school-house and site, furniture, etc., under color of a void attempt to dissolve the district to which such school-house, etc., belongs. *Ibid.*

¶45. Under Howell's Statutes §5041, providing that school districts cannot be divided or consolidated without the consent of a majority of the resident tax-payers of each district, a return by the board of school inspectors, stating that the persons consenting are a majority of the resident tax-payers of the districts, is conclusive as to such fact, though the consent filed by the districts does not state that the persons are a majority. *Gentle v. Board of School Inspectors of Colfax Township*, 40 N. W. Rep., 928.

¶46. Proceedings for organizing a new school district, taken without giving the full ten days' notice required by Howell's Statutes §5040, are not rendered valid by the filing of a consent by a majority of the citizens of each district affected, such consent being required by §5041, as the notice is a jurisdictional requirement, and the minority have a right to be heard, and a right to the full notice required. *Ibid.*

¶47. *Quo warranto* is the proper remedy to determine the legal existence of a school district, and the right of particular persons to exercise the offices of moderator, assessor, and director. *People ex rel., Roeser et al., v. Gartland, Moderator, et al.*, 42 N. W. Rep., 687.

► ¶48. Under Howell's Statutes §5033, providing that no school district shall contain more than nine sections of land, a district containing five full sections and eight fractional sections, the whole not exceeding in quantity of land nine full sections, is legal. *Ibid.*

¶49. The statutory provision concerning the election of school district officers by ballot is mandatory, but where such officers have been unanimously elected by *vive voce* vote at a regular meeting, no other persons claim to have been elected, and they are qualified and are acting, they will not be ousted by *quo warranto*. *Ibid.*

V.

DISTRICT MONEYS, WARRANTS, AND ORDERS.

¶50. An action for money had and received will lie in favor of a school district to recover district moneys received by its assessor, and which after expiration of his term of office he refuses on demand to pay over to his successor, and an action upon the assessor's bond is not the exclusive remedy; the bond is required as additional security, but it does not supersede the officer's individual responsibility. *Mason v. Fractional School District No. 1 of Scio and Webster*, 34 Mich., 228.

¶51. An assessor cannot lawfully withhold the district funds in his hands, when the same are properly demanded by his successor, a fortnight after the latter has been regularly elected and has accepted and qualified, upon any claim that he is entitled to be first personally notified officially of such election and acceptance; he is chargeable with notice of these facts without any personal certification thereof. *Ibid.*

¶52. An official treasurer cannot defend an action to make him turn over to his successor the funds in his official custody, upon any questions of the regularity of the proceedings whereby the funds came into his possession. *Ibid.*

¶53. The assessor of a school district is the lawful treasurer and depository of school district funds, and all moneys must pass through his hands and be paid out by him on proper orders. *School District No. 9 of Midland v. School District No. 5 of Midland*, 40 Mich., 551.

¶54. A showing of a want of funds is a complete answer to an application for *mandamus* to require an assessor of a school district to pay an order drawn on him in favor of a school teacher. *Allen v. Frink*, 32 Mich., 96.

¶55. It is not necessarily the duty of the moderator of a school district to countersign an order upon the assessor drawn by the director. He has a right to satisfy himself that the claim for which it was drawn is a valid one, and that it was drawn by the director in the proper performance of his duty. *Stockwell v. Township Board of White Lake*, 22 Mich., 341.

¶56. The disbursement of all school moneys is required by the statute to be made by orders drawn on the assessor by the director and countersigned by the moderator; and all moneys belonging to the district in the town treasurer's hands are required to be paid to the assessor on warrants dawn by the director and countersigned by the moderator. The assessor is made treasurer of the district, and required to hold all district moneys until properly drawn out by warrant. It is made the express duty of the director to draw and sign warrants upon the township treasurer, payable to the assessor, for all moneys raised for district purposes, or apportioned to the district by the township clerk, and present them to the moderator to be signed; and it is made the duty of the moderator to countersign such warrants. *Burns v. Bender*, 36 Mich., 195.

¶57. District moneys in the hands of the town treasurer are not subject to be applied to any district purpose except through the hands of the assessor. And the duty of suing to thus transfer them into the custody of the assessor, if qualified, is laid on the director; and the duty of procuring this transfer within some reasonable time is not discretionary, but absolute. The moderator is bound under ordinary circumstances to countersign all orders of the director for that purpose; and if he refuses in a proper case to do so, *mandamus* will lie to compel him. *Ibid.*

¶58. The statute making it the duty of the director to present the warrant to the moderator for signature, he may properly be a relator to obtain it by compulsion of law when refused. He is the proper custodian of the completed warrant, for the purpose of delivery to the assessor. *Ibid.*

¶59. The query is suggested, whether the assessor would not also be a competent relator. *Ibid.*

¶60. The town treasurer has no authority to make payments of district moneys even to the assessor, except upon the warrant prescribed by statute; and no payment not authorized by warrant is a valid official payment, such as to preclude the district from holding him responsible for moneys lawfully in his hands. Payments made otherwise than in the prescribed mode are made in his own wrong, and cannot diminish the fund for which he is responsible. *Ibid.*

¶61. Respondent occupying the double position of moderator and town treasurer, is not thereby authorized to set up his previous illegal disbursements of the district moneys as treasurer as an excuse for not doing his duty as moderator; his double functions will not relieve him in one capacity from doing his duty in another. *Ibid.*

¶62. Warrants drawn by the officers of school districts upon the township treasurer for school moneys are not negotiable, and the treasurer is under no obligation to pay them except to the district assessor. *Fox v. Shipman*, 19 Mich., 218.

¶63. An order drawn upon the township treasurer by the director and countersigned by the moderator of a school district, payable to A, or bearer, is void upon its face. The director has no power to draw any order on the township treasurer for any money of the district in his hands, payable to any one but the district assessor, who is the disbursing officer of the district. *Fractional School District No. 4 of Macomb and Chesterfield v. Mallary*, 23 Mich., 111.

¶64. The statute expressly requiring the township treasurer to pay the amount of taxes raised for school purposes to the order of the school district officers, his liability therefor is distinct from his ordinary liability for township moneys, and cannot be released or in any way affected by the action of the township board. *Jones v. Wright*, 34 Mich., 371.

¶65. A township treasurer has no right to receive for school moneys anything which the law has not authorized to be so received, and if he chooses to do so and to receipt for the taxes, he must make good the amount. *Ibid.*

¶66. A town treasurer can pay school moneys only to the school district assessor, and then only on the warrant of the proper district officers. *School District No. 9 of Midland v. School District No. 5 of Midland*, 40 Mich., 551.

¶67. A school district at an annual meeting may lawfully recognize and pay equitable claims, even though they are not strictly legal demands, against it. *Stockdale v. School District No. 2 of Wayland et al.*, 47 Mich., 226.

¶68. A vote to issue school district bonds in settlement of a demand, if in excess of the limit fixed by law, may be sustained up to the legal limit. *Ibid.*

¶69. A corporate act which can only be taken by a two-thirds vote, cannot be rescinded by a bare majority. *Ibid.*

¶70. School orders, payable to bearer, when sold, without indorsement, at a discount, and it not appearing that the vendor was asked or made any representations as to their character or consideration, it was held that in the absence of false representations or of fraud, the purchasers took them for what they were worth, and had no cause of action against the vendor. *White et al. v. Robinson*, 50 Mich., 73.

¶71. A *mandamus* will lie to compel a township treasurer to pay to the assessor of a school district so much of the money in his hands as is covered by the warrant of the director of the district drawn in favor of the assessor and in proper form, even though it does not specify a precise sum but is for all such money in his hands as was raised for the purposes of the school district and belonged thereto. *Bryant v. Moore*, 50 Mich., 225.

¶72. The custodian of public funds is bound to make payments on a proper warrant to the extent of the moneys lawfully in his hands, and cannot refuse on the ground that his right to the custody of the remainder is disputed. *Ibid.*

¶73. *Mandamus* to compel the payment of money may be granted so far as concerns a portion of the demand, while as to the rest the application is dismissed. *Ibid.*

¶74. When the moderator and assessor of a school district are sued upon an order signed by them, a finding that it was signed on a false and fraudulent statement that the school director approved and would sign it, and on condition that it should be of no force unless he did sign it, and the farther finding that there was no purpose to contract except for the district, defeats an action thereon in the absence of any showing of subsequent action creating contract relations, or of any action by defendants, taken with a knowledge of the facts and estopping them personally. *Kane v. Stowe*, 50 Mich., 317.

¶75. *Mandamus* to compel a school district assessor to pay a school order was allowed where the court was satisfied there was no valid defense. *Martin v. Tripp*, 51 Mich., 184.

¶76. Interest from the time of demand may be allowed in granting *mandamus* for the payment of a school order when it is such a settled demand as would sustain a recovery of interest at law. *Ibid.*

¶77. *Mandamus* will lie on relation of a school district assessor to compel the clerk of a township to which the district formerly belonged, to certify to the supervisor of the township to which it now belongs the amount ascertained by the school inspectors as due to the new district from what remained of the old district out of which it was erected. *Ramsey v. Clerk of Everett Township*, 52 Mich., 344.

¶78. A town treasurer refusing to pay a warrant drawn in favor of the assessor, whose official character is not questioned, on the ground that the moderator, who has been recognized as such by the other district officers, is not a legal officer, assumes a serious responsibility. The court issued a *mandamus* requiring the town treasurer to pay the order. *School District No. 8 of Tallmadge Township v. Root, Town Treasurer*, 61 Mich., 373.

VI.

TEACHERS' CONTRACTS AND CERTIFICATES.

¶79. When a contract for hiring a teacher has been signed by the director of the school district and by the teacher, and the moderator writes upon it "approved," and subscribes it as moderator, such approval and signature will be treated as in legal effect a signature of the contract by such moderator. *Everett v. Fractional School District No. 2 of Cannon*, 30 Mich., 249.

¶80. The provision of the statute that the contract for hiring a school teacher shall require the teacher to keep a correct list of the pupils, and the age of each attending the school, etc., imposes the duty upon the teacher of keeping such list, and this becomes in legal effect a part of his contract, whether the written contract expressly stipulates for it or not. *Ibid.*

¶81. The provision of the statute requiring the keeping of a list of pupils, etc., to be inserted in the contract is merely directory, and does not render invalid a contract from which such requirement has been omitted, provided it be good in other respects and entered into in good faith. *Ibid.*

¶82. A school district is a municipal corporation and cannot be garnished even by its own consent, unless the debtor also consents. *School District No. 4 of Marathon v. Gage*, 39 Mich., 484.

¶83. It is against public policy to allow the wages of persons in public employments to be reached by garnishment. *Ibid.*

¶84. School management should always conform to those decent usages which recognize the propriety of omitting to hold public exercises on recognized holidays; and it is not lawful to impose forfeitures or deductions for such proper suspension of labor. All contracts for teaching during periods mentioned must be construed of necessity as subject to such days of vacation, and there can be no penalty laid upon such observances, in the way of forfeitures or deductions of wages. *School District No. 4 of Marathon v. Gage*, 39 Mich., 484. [NOTE.—The legal holidays established by statute are New

Year's day (January 1), Washington's birth-day (February 22), Decoration day (May 30), Independence day (July 4), Christmas day (December 25), and any day appointed by the president or governor as a day of fasting and prayer, or of general thanksgiving. Whenever a legal holiday falls on Sunday, the Monday next succeeding is to be observed instead. *Act No. 124, Laws of 1865, as amended by Act No. 163, Laws of 1875, and Act No. 208, Laws of 1881.*]

¶85. If a teacher is employed for a definite time, and, during the period of his employment, the district officers close the schools on account of the prevalance of contagious diseases, and keep them closed for a time, and the teacher continues ready to perform his contract, he is entitled to full wages during such period. The act of God is not an excuse for non-performance of a contract unless it renders performance impossible; if it merely makes it difficult and inexpedient, it is not sufficient. Although under such circumstances it is eminently prudent to dismiss school, yet this affords no reason why the misfortune of the district should be visited upon the teacher. *Dewey v. Union School District of Alpena*, 43 Mich., 480.

¶86. The statute empowers the board of trustees of a graded school district to employ all teachers necessary, and what teachers are necessary is left to be decided by the sound discretion of the trustees. The making of a contract with a teacher is within the authority of a board of trustees, and, when made, neither the trustees nor the voters at an annual meeting have power to impair its obligation. *Tappan v. School District No. 1 of Carrollton*, 44 Mich., 500.

¶87. In a suit by a teacher on a contract, the plaintiff is not bound to produce the contract as proof of her certificate of qualification, and it is not error to allow her to give parol proof that she has one. *School District No. 1 of Manistee Township v. Cook*, 47 Mich., 112.

¶88. In an action by a teacher on a contract, where it was alleged as error that the contract was allowed in evidence without proof that those who acted for the school district in making it were not authorized, it was held that this allegation did not sufficiently present the objection that the officers of the district were not competent to bind it by a contract extending beyond the current year, especially as there was evidence that the officers were in possession and presumptively competent, and there was no evidence that they were not authorized to employ teachers. *Ibid.*

¶89. A school teacher cannot be lawfully employed excepting at a meeting of the board. *Hazen v. Lerche*, 47 Mich., 626.

¶90. A contract with a teacher, if signed by a majority of the board, is presumptively valid on its face and admissible in evidence without further proof. The payment by the assessor, without objection, of orders drawn on him by the director and moderator for salary of teacher estops the district from denying validity of contract under which such services were rendered, and amounts to a ratification of the contract, and direct proceedings by the district board are not essential to such ratification. *Crane v. School District No. 6 of Bennington Township*, 61 Mich., 299.

¶91. A teacher's contract is sufficiently executed if signed by the director and assessor. Simultaneous signing is not necessary. *Halloway v. School District No. 9 of Ogden Township*, 62 Mich., 153.

¶92. School district officers should know under what authority a teacher assumes to act, and cannot, by failing to hold meetings, set up their own wrong as a defense to an honest claim. A contract signed by the required number of officers, under which the teacher is permitted to teach with knowledge of the entire board, will be presumed valid. A contract valid on its face and fully performed, with acquiesence of all concerned, cannot be repudiated. *Ibid.*

¶93. Although Howell's Statutes §4969, declares that a certificate from the state normal school shall serve as a certificate of legal qualification to teach when filed in the county, city, township or district, failure to file it until after making a contract to teach is no defense to an action for salary earned after it was filed. *Smith v. School District No. 2 of Pleasant Plains,* 39 N. W. Rep., 567.

¶94. The general policy of the school law is that schools shall be taught by qualified teachers, but necessities may arise where this cannot be done. A district may be unable to find a qualified teacher. Where the employment of an unqualified teacher is a necessity, the school district is authorized to employ one who has not the proper certificate, if the school board are satisfied that the teacher is otherwise qualified, and to pay such teacher out of the moneys belonging to the district. But the primary school moneys and mill tax cannot be applied to that purpose. *State ex rel. Hale v. Risley, Moderator,* 37 N. W. Rep., 570.

¶95. Under Howell's Statutes §5154, which provides that the secretary of the board of school examiners shall have power to grant special certificates of qualification to teachers, which shall not continue in force beyond the next public examination by the board, the secretary has no power four days after such examination, to grant a special certificate to a person who had been teaching under a special certificate granted by the secretary, but who failed to pass the public examination. *Lee v. School District No. 2 of Alcona Township,* 38 N. W. Rep., 867.

¶96. The fact that a third person, at a public examination of teachers, acted with a majority of the board of examiners in conducting the examination, does not invalidate the proceedings, and a person who failed to pass cannot complain where it does not appear that such third person had anything to do with her failure to get a certificate. *Ibid.*

VII.

LIABILITIES OF DISTRICTS.

¶97. The director of a school district is not legally entitled to compensation from the district for his services. *Hinman v. School District No. 1,* 4 Mich., 168. [NOTE.—The law is since changed so as to authorize compensation to be voted by the district. *General School Laws of 1889,* § 27.]

¶98. Where two districts are united under the statute, the new district is alone liable for all the former debts of each; and a judgment afterwards rendered against one of the former districts is a nullity. *Brewer v. Palmer,* 13 Mich., 104.

¶99. Charts or cards containing the multiplication table, practical forms of business contracts, and also brief mention of prominent historical events, and designed for use in school-rooms, are held not to be necessary appendages for the school-house, within the meaning of the statute, such as the director is required to provide. *Gibson v. School District No. 5 of Vevay,* 36 Mich., 404.

¶100. There was no such necessity for the purchase of these charts as would bring the case within the principles of *School District v. Snell* (See ¶103), 24 Mich., 350. *Ibid.*

¶101. The purchase of these charts by the director, without instruction from the district board, being unauthorized and void as to the district, his retention of them, and occasionally placing them in the school-house, could not operate as a ratification by the district of his unauthorized purchase. *Ibid.*

¶102. Orders due from one district to another are not enforceable by *mandamus* at the suit of one to whom they have been assigned. *Maltz v. Board of Education,* 41 Mich., 547.

¶103. Where the officers of a school district purchased for the district a set of bound books and some blanks, suitable for the purposes of the district, at their fair value, and while the district was not properly supplied with such materials, in the absence of any showing that the discretion of such officers was abused or exceeded, the district is liable. *School District No. 4 of Easton v. Snell,* 24 Mich., 350.

¶104. One school district that has wrongfully received money belonging to another cannot, in an action by the latter to recover it, require any strict proof of the regularity of the proceedings authorizing it to be collected. *School District No. 9 of Midland v. School District No. 5 of Midland,* 40 Mich., 551.

¶105. Where a school district is parceled out among three other existing districts, the latter cannot be held jointly liable for a debt of the former district; whatever they are bound to pay must be a several, and not a joint obligation. *Halbert v. School Dists., etc.,* 36 Mich., 421.

¶106. The statute having confided the management of suits brought against a school district to the assessor when no other direction has been given by the voters in district meeting, the moderator and director, though constituting a majority of the district board, have no authority to take the defense of a suit from the assessor; the control of suits is not among the powers or duties confided by the statutes to the district board. *School District No. 4 of Rush v. Wing,* 30 Mich., 351.

¶107. The suggestion that the action of the assessor in this case was such as to be evidence of an adverse interest is disregarded; such a suggestion might be made in any case where the assessor had refused to yield his legal authority to another. *Ibid.*

¶108. A judgment for costs against the district on the dismissal of an appeal taken in the name of the district by the director, without the authority or assent of the assessor, on the ground that the district had not appealed, is held to be erroneous. *Ibid.*

¶109. Costs are not awarded against the school district in this court, on a writ of error brought without authority of the assessor, to review such dismissal. *Ibid.*

¶110. A *mandamus* will lie to compel a school district to pay orders issued by it, even though the district has since been subdivided, where statutory provision for distributing the original liability has not been carried out. *Turnbull v. Board of Education,* 45 Mich., 496.

¶111. Interest upon orders issued by a school district is denied upon granting a *mandamus* to compel their payment if no authority has been given to impose it. *Ibid.*

VIII.

TUITION OF NON-RESIDENT PUPILS.

¶112. Before any action can be maintained under the statutes, for the tuition of non-resident pupils, the district board must first fix and determine the rate of tuition of such pupils; and this should be by resolution of the board, properly recorded by the director in the records of the district; and the fact that such action has been taken, cannot be shown by parol, if objected to. *Thompson v. School District No. 6 of Crockery*, 25 Mich., 483.

IX.

ADMISSION OF COLORED CHILDREN TO SCHOOL.

¶113. The amendment to the primary school law of 1867—Laws of 1867, vol. 1, p. 42 [*General 'School Laws of 1889*, § 45,]—giving equal rights in the schools to all residents, is applicable to the city of Detroit, and precludes the board of education of that city from excluding a child from any public school on the ground of color. *People v. Board of Education*, 18 Mich., 400.

X.

SCHOOL SITES AND SCHOOL-HOUSES.

¶114. Notice of a meeting of the board of school inspectors to change a school-house site is necessary. *Andress v. School Inspectors of Williamstown*, 19 Mich., 332. (See ¶1 preceding.)

¶115. The board of inspectors have no power to change a school-house site on a written request of a majority of qualified voters of the district except in cases where the site has been fixed by them because the inhabitants were unable to agree upon a site. *Ibid.*

¶116. The jurisdiction to condemn lands for a school-house site is invoked by presenting to the proper officer a petition designating the site and showing disagreement with the owner as to compensation for it. *Smith v. School District No. 2 of Milton*, 40 Mich., 143.

¶117. In proceedings to condemn land for a school-house site, the circuit judge is not required to act in preference to a circuit court commissioner. *Ibid.*

¶118. When the owner of land that is sought for a school-house site is represented at the proceedings to condemn it, he is deemed to waive objection to jurors if he does not challenge them at the time. *Ibid.*

¶119. When the petition, notice, *venire*, finding and commissioner's certificate in proceedings to condemn land for a school-house site are regular on their face, and show full compliance with statutory requirements, the proceedings are presumed regular, and if the parties interested were represented, and omit, on filing the proceedings, to make a sworn showing to the circuit court of any other defects—such as an omission to designate the site to the jury—they cannot rely on it thereafter. *Ibid.*

¶120. A school district contracting for the building of school-house within a stated time, is bound to furnish a suitable site therefor within such reasonable time that the constructors shall not be delayed on their part. *Todd et al. v. School District No. 1 of Greenwood,* 40 Mich., 294.

¶121. Under a contract for the construction of a school building, which provides that the work shall be "executed in the best and most workmanlike manner, and agreeably to such directions as may be given from time to time" by the architect or his assistant [the local superintendent of the work, employed by the district], "and to his full and entire satisfaction, without reference thereon to any other person;" that all claims for alterations or extras were to be judged of, determined, and adjusted "solely by the superintendent," and that payment should be made on the certificate of the architect, or superintendent, partly on monthly estimates, from time to time, and the balance on completion of the building; whatever passed under the inspection of the superintendent as the work progressed, and was in good faith approved by him, expressly or by implication, was not open to objection on the part of the district afterwards; and the certificate of the architect was not a condition precedent to the right of the contractor to recover for the work so approved. *Wilday v. Fractional School District No. 1 of Paw Paw and Antwerp,* 25 Mich., 419.

¶122. Variances from such a contract which have been treated at the time as immaterial by both parties will not afterwards be held to be departures from the contract; and what was regarded at the time as substantial compliance with its terms, constitutes a performance in law. *Ibid.*

¶123. Intentional departures from such contract, made without the consent, express or implied, of the district officers, architect, or superintendent, and in disregard of their directions, would not bar a recovery for other portions of the work which were duly approved; but the district would have a right to insist on the proper changes in the work to make it conform to the contract, and to recover any damages sustained by the failure. *Ibid.*

¶124. The mere fact of taking possession and occupying the building by the district for their schools, after the time when, by the contract, it was to be completed, would not, of itself, constitute an acceptance which should bar any claim on the part of the district to insist upon a rectification of any faults, or the payment of any damages they may have suffered by the failure in strict compliance; but the fact of making payments afterward without objection, the manner of taking possession, and whether with or without objection to any variation, would have an important bearing on the question of fact, whether any rights were intentionally waived, or whether there was a purpose to accept the building as completed in substantial compliance with the contract. *Ibid.*

¶125. *Mandamus* will not lie to compel a circuit judge to overrule his finding that the proceedings taking for the condemnation of a site for a school-house were irregular, and to compel him to enter judgment for the amount found due. *School District No. 5 of the Township of Delhi v. The Circuit Judge for Ingham County,* 49 Mich., 432.

¶126. Proceedings to condemn land for a school-house site will be quashed if there is no lawful designation thereof shown by the records. *Heck v. School District No. 2 of Essex*, 49 Mich., 551.

¶127. The school law (Act 164 of 1881) permits land to be condemned for school purposes only when a site has been lawfully determined, and it confines the power of the township inspectors to determine the site to cases where the inhabitants themselves cannot do it. And it seems that more than one site cannot be designated except by the inhabitants. *Ibid.*

¶129. The justice to whom a petition for the condemnation of land for a school-house site is presented, is not empowered to hear evidence or pass on any of the merits. *Ibid.*

¶130. Where proceedings to condemn land for a school-house site are brought before a jury, proof of a legal selection of a site must be made to them, and without it they cannot find it to be necessary to condemn it. *Ibid.*

¶131. A lease to a school district, to hold the property "during the time it is used for school purposes," is a lease in perpetuity at the will of the lessee; and as the lessee is a corporation, and words of inheritance are not required, the lease, if a present consideration is paid, really operates as a bargain and sale, and conveys a base or determinable fee. This is sufficient to satisfy the provisions of the school law, which requires a title in fee or a lease for ninety-nine years where land is to be secured for erecting a stone or brick school-house. *School District No. 5 of Delhi v. Everett*, 52 Mich., 314.

¶132. After the lapse of a dozen years it is too late to disturb the title to a school-house site by mere questions of regularity in the proceedings to designate it. *Ibid.*

¶133. A *surety* on a bond given to secure the performance of a contract for building a school-house cannot recover of the trustees of the district for moneys due him for materials furnished in the erection of the building, by reason of their failure to require the contractor to execute the statutory bond provided for by act No. 94, Laws of 1883. *Owen v. Hill et al.*, 67 Mich., 43.

¶134. Whether such trustees are liable *in any event* for such neglect of duty, query,—Sherwood and Champlin, J. J., holding them so liable, and Campbell, C. J., and Morse, J., reserving their opinion on the subject. *Ibid.*

XI.

GRADED AND HIGH SCHOOLS.

¶135. The right of school authorities in union school districts of this State to levy taxes upon the general public for the support of high schools, and by such taxation to make free the instruction of children in other languages than English, is sustained. *Stuart v. School District No. 1 of Kalamazoo*, 30 Mich., 69.

¶136. A school district which has assumed to possess and exercise all the rights and franchises of a regularly organized corporation for thirteen years, with entire acquiescence of everybody, is not liable to have the regularity of its organization, or of the legislation under which it acted, called in question thereafter in a merely private and collateral suit. *Ibid.*

11

¶137. Whether or not the statute of limitations applies in terms to a case where it is not so much the organization of the school district that is questioned as its authority to establish a high school and levy taxes therefor, it is strictly applicable in principle. *Ibid.*

¶138. The organization claimed and asserted by the district being that of a union school district, the presumption of organization arising from its user of corporate power must be that of such an organization as its user indicates, and whether or not an acquiescence for the statutory period of two years will raise the presumption of regular organization, one of thirteen years certainly will. *Ibid.*

¶139. The State policy of Michigan on the subject of education, and of the territory before the State was organized, beginning in 1817 and continuing down until after the adoption of the present constitution, having been reviewed and considered, the conclusion is reached that there is nothing in our State policy, or in our constitution, or in our laws, restricting the primary school districts of the State in the branches of knowledge which their officers may cause to be taught, or the grade of instruction that may be given, if the voters of the district consent in regular form to bear the expense and raise the taxes for the purpose, or to prevent instruction in the classics and living modern languages in these schools. *Ibid.*

¶140. The power to make the appointment of a superintendent of schools in a union school district is one that is incident to the full control which by law the district board has over the schools of the district. *Ibid.*

¶141. The decree below, dismissing the bill filed in this case to restrain the collection of such portion of the school taxes assessed against the complainants for the year 1872 as has been voted for the support of the high school in the village of Kalamazoo and for the payment of the salary of the superintendent, is affirmed. *Ibid.*

¶142. The board of trustees of a graded school have authority to purchase a piano for the purposes of a high school. *Knabe et al. v. The Board of Education of the City of West Bay City*, 67 Mich., 262.

¶143. When the law gives the board of trustees power to prescribe the course of studies, it gives them the authority to provide *means* to carry the power into effect. *Ibid.*

XII.

LIBRARY MONEYS.

¶144. The treasurer of the board of school inspectors, and not the township treasurer, is the proper custodian of the township library money; and the latter officer, on proper demand, is bound to pay it over to the former, and is not entitled to withhold it until it is drawn by the inspectors as needed for specific appropriations; and *mandamus* will lie to enforce the performance of this duty. *McPharlin v. Mahoney*, 30 Mich., 100.

¶145. It is a sufficient ground for an application for *mandamus* to enforce such payment, that the township treasurer, when an order was properly drawn on him by the inspectors for such money, but for an amount slightly in excess of the money in his hands, refused to pay over what he had, not upon the ground that the order was too large a sum, but upon the distinct assertion that he was himself the proper custodian of the funds, and was not bound to pay them over except as they were required by the inspectors for specific purposes. *Ibid.*

¶146. Under the constitution and statutes, all moneys which are paid into the office of the county treasurer, on account of fines, penalties, forfeitures and recognizances, are to be credited to the library fund, and apportioned and paid over by the treasurer to the proper local officers, without any deduction for expenses, either attending the collection of the particular sums paid in, or embracing the general criminal expenses of the county. *Board of Education of Detroit v. Treasurer of Wayne County*, 8 Mich., 392.

XIII.

MISCELLANEOUS.

¶147. A communication, representing that a certain person was of bad moral character, and wholly unfit to teach and have the care of a district school, made to a township superintendent by persons interested in a particular school within his jurisdiction, for the sole purpose of preventing the issue to the person so charged of a license to teach the school, is held to be a privileged communication, and not actionable. *Wieman v. Mabee*, 45 Mich., 484.

¶148. An action will not lie on a communication relating to personal character, if made in good faith and for an honest purpose by persons concerned, and to the proper person. Nor will it lie when such a communication is untrue, if it is not maliciously made. *Ibid.*

¶149. A school director has authority, in the exercise of a sound discretion, to buy new seats for a school-house under a resolution adopted at the annual meeting of the school district "that the school board fix the school-house ready for the winter term." *McLaren v. Town Board of Akron*, 48 Mich., 189.

¶150. Act 164 of 1881, in authorizing the removal of a school district officer for illegally using or disposing of any of the public moneys entrusted to his care, does not cover a charge of conspiring with a woman moderator to hire her husband as teacher and pay him more than was necessary to obtain a good teacher. *Ibid.*

¶151. If one of two parties claiming the office of moderator obtains a judgment of ouster against co-claimant and is recognized by the director and assessor, he becomes an incumbent of the office *de facto*, and his action will be respected while in office. *School District No. 8 of Tallmadge Township v. Root, Town Treasurer*, 61 Mich., 373.

¶152. The practice of taking "informal ballots" at regular elections has no legal sanction, may mislead voters and is open to grave abuse and is so held when indulged in at annual school meeting. *Ibid.*

¶153. A line fence around the school-house site is a "necessary appendage" within the meaning of the statute. "Appendages" under the school statutes, includes fuel, fences, and necessary out-houses. The duty of the director to provide the same is not confined to the school term. They should be on hand when the school opens. It then becomes his duty to keep the same in repair, as also the school-house. *Creager v. School District No. 9 of Wright Township*, 62 Mich., 101.

¶154. Direction for the payment of primary school money apportioned by the superintendent of public instruction as between districts, if accompanying the apportionment, cannot be altered or modified by the town clerk. *Moiles, Assessor v. Watson, Treasurer, &c.,* 60 Mich., 415.

¶155. Title of *de facto* officer will not be tried on application for *mandamus. Ibid.*

¶156. The mother of a child included in the school census of the district, who had resided therein more than three months, and was more than twenty-one years of age, was entitled to vote at a school meeting for school trustees, though the constitution of Michigan limits the right of suffrage to males, as the constitutional qualifications do not apply to officers for which the legislature has the right to provide, among which are school trustees. *Belles v. Burr et al.,* 43 N. W. Rep., 24.

(NOTE—This decision does not apply to cities whose charters provide that school officers shall be voted for on the same ballot with other municipal officers at a general election. See *Mudge v. Jones,* 59 Mich., 165.)

¶157. A rule by a school board that "pupils who shall in any way deface or injure the school building, out houses, furniture, maps or anything else belonging to the school, shall be suspended from school until full satisfaction is made" will not be enforced against a boy who accidentally breaks a window glass. Such a rule will not be sustained where the act was done merely through carelessness or negligence, but it must be wilful or malicious to warrant suspension from school. *Joseph H. Holman v. Trustees of District No. 5, Township of Avon.* Opinion filed Nov. 8, 1889.

APPENDIX B.

———

FORMS FOR PROCEEDINGS UNDER THE SCHOOL LAWS.

———

NOTE.—The following blank forms do not comprise a full set for all purposes under the school laws. All furnished by the Superintendent of Public Instruction, together with such as may be required in proceedings where the services of attorneys are usually employed, and a few for which those published may be readily adapted, are omitted. Officers are advised, when performing any duty to which these forms are applicable, to use them in preference to others, as by this means uniformity of administration is secured, many mistakes will be prevented, and in time that which may now seem complicated and obscure will be more generally understood.

FORM No. 1.

Notice by the Clerk of the Board of Inspectors to a Taxable Inhabitant of a District at the Time of its Formation.

[See Compiler's Sections 9 and 10.]

To A......B......:

SIR—The board of school inspectors of the township of.............have formed a school district in said township, to be known as district No. ...., and bounded as follows: [Here insert the description.]

The first meeting of said district will be held at..............on the....day of ...., 18...., at......o'clock......M., and you are instructed to notify every legal voter of said district of the same, at least five days previous to said meeting, either personally, or by leaving a written notice at his place of residence. You will indorse on this notice a return, showing each notification, with the date or dates thereof, and deliver the same to the chairman of said meeting.

Dated this........day of............, 18....
    (Signed,)
                                 C.......D........,
                          Clerk of the Board of School Inspectors.

———

FORM No. 2.

Notice of First Meeting—when made in writing to be left at the house of every legal voter.

[See Compiler's Sections 9, 10, and 24.]

To C.......D........:

SIR—School district No....., of the township of..........., having been formed by the board of school inspectors, you, as a legal voter in said district, are hereby notified that the first meeting thereof will be held at.................., on the......day of..........., 18..., at....o'clock....M.

Dated this......day of............, 18...
    (Signed,)
                              A.......B........
                     [The person appointed to give notice.]

FORM NO. 3.

Endorsement upon the notice (Form No. 1) by Taxable Inhabitant.

[See Compiler's Sections 9, 10, 24, and 139.]

I, A..... B......, hereby return the within (or annexed) notice, having notified the qualified voters of the district, as follows:

NAMES.	DATE.	HOW NOTIFIED
A..... B........................	January 1, 1882..........	Personally.
C.. .. D........................	" 1, 1882..........	Written Notice.
E..... F........................	" 2, 1882..........	Personally.

Dated this........day of..............., 18...
(Signed,)   A............. B.............

FORM NO. 4.

Notice by Township Clerk to Director, of Alteration in District.

[See Compiler's Section 18.]

To the Director of School District No......., Township of.............:

SIR—At a meeting of the board of school inspectors of the township of..............., held..............., 18..., the boundaries of school district No.........., township of ...., were altered in such manner that the territory of said district now includes the following: [Here insert the description.]

Dated this........day of..............., 18....
(Signed,)   C............D............,
Clerk of the Board of School Inspectors.

FORM NO. 5.

Acceptance of Office by District Officers, to be filed with the Director.

[See Compiler's Sections 32, 108, and 140.]

I do hereby accept the office of.........................in school district No.........., of the township of.....................

Dated this........day of............., 18...
(Signed,)   A............. B.............

FORM NO. 6.

Assessor's Bond.

[See Compiler's Section 52.]

KNOW ALL MEN BY THESE PRESENTS: That we, A............B............, assessor of school district No. ...., township of................., county of.................,

and State of Michigan, C........... D........... and E........... F...........
[his sureties], are held firmly bound unto said district in the sum of.... ....
[here insert double the amount expected to c me into the assessor's hands], to be paid
to the said district ; for the payment of which sum well and truly to be made, we bind
ourselves, our heirs, executors and administrators, jointly and severally, firmly by
these presents.

The condition of the above obligation is such that if the said......................
...............assessor as aforesaid, shall faithfully discharge the duties of his office
as assessor of said school district, and shall well and truly pay over to the person or
persons entitled thereto, upon the proper order therefor, all sums of money which
shall come into his hands as assessor of said district, and shall, at the expiration of his
term of office, pay over to his successor in office all moneys remaining in his hands as
assessor aforesaid, and shall deliver to his successor all books and papers appertaining
to his said office, then this obligation shall be void, otherwise of full force and virtue.

Sealed with our seals, and dated this......day of...........18...

A........... B............., [L. S.]
C........... D............., [L. S.]
E.......... F............., [L. S.]

Signed, sealed, and delivered in presence of
....
....

We approve the within bond.
(Signed,)   G .... H............., *Moderator.*
                                J........... K............., *Director.*

FORM No. 7.

Notice of Annual Meeting.

[See Compiler's Sections 21, 23, and 48.]

NOTICE.—The annual meeting of school district No. ...., of the township of........
..........., for the election of school district officers, and for the transaction of such
other business as may lawfully come before it, will be held at ...., on Monday, the .... day of September [or July], 18.., at .... o'clock ..M.

Dated this ...... day of August [or July], 18...

(Signed,)   A........... B............., *Director.*

FORM No. 8.

Request to be made by five Legal Voters of a District to the District Board for a Special Meeting.

[See Compiler's Section 22.]

To the District Board of School District No. .... (or to A......... B........., one of the District Board):

The undersigned, legal voters of school district No. ...., of the township of
......................, request you, in pursuance of section 15 of chapter II of the
general school laws of 1889, to call a special meeting of said district, for the purpose of
....

Dated this .... day of ...., 18...

(Signed,)

C........... D............,
E........... F............,
G........... H............,
I........... K............,
L........... M............,

FORM NO. 9.

Notice of Special Meeting.

[See Compiler's Sections 22 and 23.]

NOTICE—A *special meeting* of the legal voters of school district No............, in the township of....................., called on the written request of five legal voters [or called by the district board, as the case may be], will be held at................, on the ....day of..................., 18..., at........o'clock....M., for the purpose of [here insert *every object* that is to be brought before the meeting].
                    (Signed,)   A............B............, *Director.*

FORM NO. 10.

Order upon the Assessor for Moneys to be disbursed by him, with Receipt attached.

[See Compiler's Sections 48 and 52.]

Assessor of School District No...:......, Township of..................:
    SIR—Pay to..............the sum of...............___dollars out of any moneys
                                                                    100
in your hands belonging to the [here insert name of fund on which order is drawn, as "teachers' wages," "building," etc.] fund, on account of [here state the object for which the order was drawn].
    Dated this........day of..................., 18...
                                        A............B............, *Director.*
        [Countersigned :]
C............D............, *Moderator.*

    Received of E...........F............, assessor of school district No....., the amount specified in the above order.
                            G..................H. ....

FORM NO. 11.

Warrant upon Township Treasurer for Moneys belonging to School District.

[See Compiler's Sections 46, 52, and 72.]

Treasurer of the Township of.....................:
    SIR—Pay to A.......... B............, assessor of school district No........, in said township the sum of....................... ....___dollars, out of [here insert the
                                                                            100
particular fund], in your hands belonging to said district.
    Dated at............, this...........day of..................18....
                                        C............D............, *Director.*
        [Countersigned :]
E...........F..........., *Moderator.*

FORM NO. 12.

Certificate by District Board to Township Clerk, of District Taxes to be Assessed.

[See Compiler's Section 37.]

Clerk of the Township of.................. ..:
    The undersigned, district board of school district No........., township of..........., do hereby certify that the following taxes have been voted by the qualified electors of

said district, during the school year last closed, and estimated and voted by the district board, under the provisions of law, viz:

For teachers' wages	$	
For building purposes		
For repairs		
For paying bonded indebtedness		
For fuel		
For library		
For apparatus		
For incidental expenses		
For		
Total	$	

Which amounts you will report to the supervisor to be assessed upon the taxable property of said district in accordance with the provisions of law.

Dated at............, this........day of........_..., 18...

A............ B............, *Moderator.*
C............ D............, *Director.*
E............ F............, *Assessor.*

FORM NO. 13.

Bond to be given by the Chairman of the Board of School Inspectors.

[See Compiler's Section 54.]

KNOW ALL MEN BY THESE PRESENTS: That we, A........ B........., the chairman of the board of school inspectors of the township of.........., county of............, and State of Michigan, and C........ D........ and E........ F.........[his sureties] are held and firmly bound unto the said township, in the sum of [here insert the sum of double the amount to come into said chairman's hands, as nearly as the same can be ascertained] for the payment of which sum well and truly to be made to the said township, we bind ourselves, our heirs, executors, and administrators, jointly and severally, firmly by these presents.

The condition of this obligation is such that if A........ B........, chairman of the board of.school inspectors, shall faithfully appropriate all moneys that may come into his hands by virtue of his office, then this obligation shall be void; otherwise, of full force and virtue.

Sealed with our seals, and dated this........day of............, 18...

A........ B........., [L.S.]
C........ D........, [L.S.]
E........ F........., [L.S.]

Signed, sealed, and delivered in the presence of

I approve the within bond.

(Signed,)   G........ H........., *Township Clerk.*

FORM NO. 14.

Appointment of District Officers by District Board.

[See Compiler's Sections 30 and 108.]

The undersigned, members of the district board of school district No. ....,
township of ...., do hereby appoint A............ B.................
[*director, moderator,* or *assessor,* as the case may be] of said district, to fill the vacancy
created by the [removal, resignation, or death, etc.] of C.......... D................,
the late incumbent.

Dated this ......day of ...., 18....

                E.......... F..........., *Moderator,*
                G......... .. H............, *Assessor.*

FORM NO. 15.

Appointment of District Officers by School Inspectors.

[See Compiler's Sections 30 and 108.]

The undersigned, school inspectors for the township of ...., do hereby
appoint A............ B............ [*director, moderator,* or *assessor,* as the case may
be] of school district No. ...., in said township; the district having failed to elect.

Dated this .... day of ...., 18....

           C.......... D..........,
           E.......... F..........,
           G.......... H..........,
                Board of School Inspectors.

FORM NO. 16.

Notice of Meeting of Inspectors.

[See Compiler's Section 15.]

NOTICE.—A meeting of the board of school inspectors of the township of...........
........, will be held at ...., on the .... day of ...., 18..., at....
o'clock ....M., for the purpose of [here insert *every object* that is to be brought before
the meeting, and if for the purpose of changing boundaries of districts, state the
alterations proposed.]

Dated this .... day of ...., 18....

                A.............. B.............,
              Clerk of the Board of School Inspectors

FORM NO. 17.

*Certificate to be given to the Director of a School District, by the Board of School
Inspectors when they establish a Site.*

[See Compiler's Section 89.]

The inhabitants of school district No. ...., township of ...., having
failed, at a legal meeting, to establish a site for a school-house, the board of school
inspectors hereby certify that they have determined that the said site shall be as follows
[here insert description.]

Given under our hands this .... day of ...., 18....

           A.......... B..........,
           C.......... D..........,
           E.......... F..........,
                Board of School Inspectors.

FORM No. 1

Warrant on the Township Treasurer for Library Moneys.

[See Compiler's Section 114.]

To the Treasurer of the Township of ...., County of ....:

SIR—Pay to ...., chairman of the board of school inspectors, the sum of ....$\frac{}{100}$ dollars, from the library moneys in your hands, or to come into your hands, the same being for the support of the library of said township.

Dated at ...., this ...... day of ...., 18....

A.......... B..............,
C.......... D..............,
E.......... F..............,
Township Board of School Inspectors.

REMARK.—In case one or more district libraries are established in a township the library moneys due such districts are payable on the order of the district officer. (See Form No. 11.)

FORM No. 19.

Notice by the Township Treasurer to the Township Clerk of Moneys to be Apportioned to Districts.

[See Compiler's Sections 72 and 73.]

To the Clerk of the Township of ...., County of ....:

SIR—I have now in my hands for apportionment to the several school districts of this township the following moneys:

Primary school interest fund...$........
Library moneys received from county treasurer............................ ....
One mill tax... ....
Surplus dog tax... ....
District taxes.. ....
Special funds... ....

Dated this .... day of ...., 18....

A.......... B..............,
Township Treasurer.

FORM No. 20.

Notice by the Township Clerk to the Township Treasurer, of the Apportionment of Moneys to Districts.

[See Compiler's Sections 63 and 64.]

To the Treasurer of the Township of............, *County of*............:

SIR—Herewith find a statement of the number of children of school age in each school district of this township, entitled to draw public moneys, and the amount of moneys apportioned to each of said districts:

DISTRICTS.	No. of Children in District.	Primary School Interest Fund.	Library Moneys.	One-mill Tax.	Surplus Dog-Tax.	District Taxes.	Special Funds.	Total to each District.
District No. 1	......	$......	$......	$.	$......	$......	$......	$ ......
District No. 2, fr'l	......	......	......	......	......	......		
......	......				......	......		
......	......						......	......
Total	......	$......	$......	$......	$......	$......	$......	$......

Dated this........day of............, 18...

A............ B............,
Township Clerk.

FORM No. 21.

Notice by the Township Clerk to Directors, of Moneys belonging to the Districts.

[See Compiler's Section 64.]

A.... B...., *Director of School District No*....., *Township of*.........:

SIR—The amount of school moneys apportioned to school district No....., township of............, is as follows:

Primary school interest fund..$........
Library moneys received from county treasurer........................... ....
One-mill tax... ....
Surplus dog-tax... ....
District taxes.. ....
Special funds.. ....

Total..$........
Dated this........day of............, 18...

A............ B............,
Township Clerk.

FORM No. 22.

Certificate by the Township Clerk to the Supervisor, of District Taxes to be Assessed.

[See Compiler's Section 62.]

Supervisor of the Township of ...., *County of* ....:

SIR—I hereby certify that the following is a correct statement of moneys proposed to be raised by taxation for school purposes in each of the several school districts of this township, as the same appears from the reports of the district boards of the several districts now on file in my office:

DISTRICTS.	For teachers' wages.	For building purposes.	For repairs.	For paying indebtedness.	For fuel.	For library.	For apparatus.	For incidental expenses.	For.......	Total.
District No. 1............	$........	$........	$........	$........	$........	$........	$........	$........	$........	$........
District No. 2, fr'l.....										
....	.. ....	....	....	....	....	....	....	....	....	....
....										

Which amounts you will assess upon the taxable property of each of said districts in accordance with the provisions of law.
Dated this .... day of ...., 18....

A.......... B............,
Township Clerk.

FORM No. 23.

Deed to School District.

[See Compiler's Section 35.]

KNOW ALL MEN BY THESE PRESENTS: That A...... B......, and C...... D......, his wife, of the township of ...., county of ...., and State of ...., party of the first part, for and in consideration of the sum of..............$\frac{}{100}$ dollars, to them paid by the district board of school district No. ...., of the township of ...., county of ...., and State of Michigan, the receipt whereof is hereby acknowledged, do hereby grant, bargain, sell, and convey to school district No. .... aforesaid, the party of the second part, and their assigns forever, the following described parcel of land, namely [here insert description]: together with all the privileges and appurtenances thereunto belonging, to have and to hold the same to the said party of the second part, and their assigns, forever. And the said party of the first part for themselves, their heirs, executors, and administrators, do covenant, grant, bargain and agree, to and with the said party of the second part, and their assigns, that at the time of the ensealing and delivery of these presents they were well seized of the premises above conveyed, as of a good, sure, perfect, absolute, and indefeasible estate of inheritance in the law, in fee simple, and that the said lands and premises are free from all encumbrances whatever; and that the above bargained premises, in the quiet and peaceable possession of the said party of the second part, and their assigns, against all and every person or persons lawfully claiming or to claim the whole or any part thereof, they will forever warrant and defend.

In witness whereof, the said A........ B........, and C........ D.... ..., his wife, party of the first part, have hereunto set their hands and seals, this .... day of ...., 18....

A.......... B............, [SEAL.]
C.......... D............, [SEAL.]

Signed, sealed, and delivered in presence of
E............ F............,
G............ H............

STATE OF ...., ⎰ ss.
County of .... ⎱

On this .... day of .... in the year one thousand eight hundred and
............, before me, I......... K........., a ...., in and for said county,
personally appeared, ..., and ...., his wife, to me known
to be the same persons described in and who executed the within instrument, who
severally acknowledged the same to be their free act and deed.

Witness my hand and official seal, the day and year last above named.

                                    I......... K........., [SEAL.]
                                    ....

FORM No. 24.

Lease to School District.

[See Compiler's Section 35.]

KNOW ALL MEN BY THESE PRESENTS: That A......... B........., of the township of..........., county of............, and State of................, of the first
part, for the consideration herein mentioned, does hereby lease unto school district
No........., in the township of..........., county of..........., and State of Michigan, party of the second part, and their assigns, the following parcel of land, to wit:
[Here insert description] with all the privileges and appurtenances thereunto belonging; to have and to hold the same for and during the term of......years from the.....
day of..........., 18.... And the said party of the second part, for themselves and
their assigns, do covenant and agree to pay the said party of the first part, for the
said premises, the annual rent of...........dollars.

In testimony whereof, the said parties have hereunto set their hands and seals, this
...........day of............, 18....

                        A......... B.........[SEAL.]
                                         Lessor.

                        C......... D........., ⎫
                        E......... F........., ⎬ [SEAL.]
                        G.........H........., ⎭

        District Board of School District No..... of the aforesaid Township.
Signed and sealed in the presence of
    I......... K.........
    L.........M.........

FORM No. 25.

Contract for Building a School-House.

[See Compiler's Section 35.]

Contract made and entered into between A......... B........., of the township of
........., in the county of........., and State of Michigan, and C......... D.........,
E......... F........., and G......... H........., composing the district board of school
district No....., of the township of..........., in the county of........., and State of
Michigan, and their successors in office.

In consideration of the sum of one dollar in hand paid, the receipt whereof is hereby
acknowledged, and of the further sum of...........dollars, to be paid as hereinafter
specified, the said A.........B......... hereby agrees to build a...........school-house,
and to furnish the material therefor, according to the plan and specifications for the
erection of said house, hereto appended, at such point in said district as said district
board may designate. The said house is to be built of the best material, in a substan-

tial, workman-like manner; and is to be completed and delivered to the said district board or their successors in office, free from any lien for work done or material furnished, by the........day of.......... 18... And in case the said house is not finished by the time herein specified, the said A........ B........ shall forfeit and pay to the said district board or their successors in office, for the use of said district, the sum of ....dollars, and shall also be liable for all damages that may result to said district in consequence of said failure.

The said district board or their successors in office, in behalf of said district, hereby agree to pay the said A........ B...... the sum of......... dollars when the foundation of said house is finished ; and the further sum of...................dollars when the walls are up and ready for the roof; and the remaining sum of.............dollars when the said house is finished and delivered as herein stipulated.

It is further agreed that this contract shall not be sub-let, transferred or assigned without the consent of both parties.

Witness our hands this........day of............., 18...

A............. B.............,
Contractor.

C............. D.............,
E............. F.............,
G............. H.............,
District Board.

FORM No. 26.

Contract between District Board and Teacher.

[See Compiler's Sections 38, 40, 56, 109, and 128.]

It is hereby contracted and agreed between the district board of school district No..... in the township of..........., county of..........., and State of Michigan, and A...... B........, a legally qualified teacher in said township, that the said A........B........ shall teach the school of said district for the term of........months, commencing on the........day of............., 18...; and the said A........B........ agrees to faithfully keep a correct list of the pupils, and the age of each attending school, and the number of days each pupil is present, and to furnish the director of the district with a correct copy of the same at the close of the school; and to observe and enforce the rules and regulations established by the district board.

The said district board, in behalf of said district, agrees to keep the school-house in good repair, to provide the necessary fuel to keep the school-house in comfortable condition, and to pay said A........B........for the said services as teacher, to be faithfully and truly rendered and performed, the sum of.............dollars per month, the same being the amount of wages above agreed upon, to be paid on or before the....... day of........., 18..: *Provided*, That in case said A........B........shall be dismissed from school, by the district board, for gross immorality, or violation of this contract, or shall permit h...certificate of qualification to expire, or shall have said certificate annulled or suspended by the county board of school examiners, or other lawful authority, h...shall not be entitled to any compensation from and after such annullment, suspension or dismissal.

In witness whereof, we have hereunto subscribed our names, this.............day of ...., 18...

C............. D........•....,)
E............. F............., > *District Board.*
G............. H.............,)
A............. B............., *Teacher.*

FORM NO. 27.

Teacher's General Register.

[See Compiler's Section 40.]

REGISTER of the School taught in District No. _____, of the township of _____, in the County of _____, and State of Michigan, for the Term commencing on the _____ day of _____, 18....., and ending on the _____ day of _____, 18.....

No.	PUPILS. NAME.	Age.	ATTENDANCE IN DAYS FOR WEEK COMMENCING								Total Attendance in Days.	STUDIES PURSUED BY EACH SCHOLAR.								
			January 6.	January 13.	January 20.	January 27.	February 3.	February 10.				Orthography.	Reading.	Writing.	Arithmetic.	Geography.	Grammar.	U. S. History.	Civil Government.	Physiology and Hygiene.
1	A............B............	7	5	3	4	5	2	4			23	*	*		*	*				*
2	C............D............	14	4	4	5	1	3	5			18		*				*	*	*	*
3	E............F............	10	3	4	4	3	5	4			23	*	*		*	*				

I hereby certify that the above is a faithful and correct register of said school.

A.............. B.............., *Teacher.*

NOTE.—The above register, properly certified by the teacher, should be filed with the Director of the District immediately after the close of the school. Each column under the head of "Attendance in Days" is designed to embrace the number of days *present* each week, and the sum of days *present* during the term given in the twentieth column to the right.

The words "for weeks commencing" (in the above form) refer to "January 6," in the left hand column under the head of "Attendance in days," etc. The star, thus *, denotes the studies pursued by each pupil. To ascertain the average number of days scholars attend school, add together the numbers of days of attendance of all the pupils (as found in 20th column) and divide this sum by the number of pupils who have attended school.

☞ The teacher should make out this *average* and indicate it upon the register for the convenience of the Director.

Under the provisions of §42, the teacher is required to certify in the register, before placing it in the hands of the Director, whether or not instruction has been given in physiology and hygiene, with special reference to the effects of alcohol and narcotics upon the human system, in the school or grade presided over by the teacher.

APPENDIX C.

RULES FOR SCHOOL LIBRARIES.

NOTE.—The following regulations for the management of school libraries are prepared in accordance with the provisions of compiler's sections 3 and 115 of the general school laws. As given, these rules are suitable for township libraries; if it be desired to adapt them to the needs of district libraries, a few slight changes, which are readily apparent, will be necessary.

1. The librarian shall have charge of the library, and keep a catalogue of all the books belonging to the library, in a book to be provided for that purpose.

2. Every volume in the library shall have pasted on the inside of the cover a printed label, giving the name of the township, the number of the volume, and the fine for not returning it within the specified time, and for the loss of or injury to any book.

3. Every volume loaned shall be entered by the librarian in a book to be provided for that purpose, by its catalogue number, with the day on which it was loaned, the name of the borrower, and the name of the person to whom it is charged (see regulation 5), the date when returned and condition of the book, and the fine assessed for detention or injury to the book, as in the following form:

Date of Delivery.	No. of book Delivered.	To whom Delivered.	To whom Charged.	When Returned.	Condition when Returned	Fine for Detention.	Fine for Injury.

4. No person shall be allowed to have more than one volume at a time, or to retain the same longer than two weeks; nor shall any person who has incurred a fine imposed by these regulations, receive a book while such fine remains unpaid.

5. Books may be loaned to minors and charged to their parents, guardians, or other persons with whom they reside, who shall be responsible for the books under these regulations.

13

6. On the election of a librarian, his predecessor shall, within ten days thereafter, deliver to him all the printed and manuscript books, pamphlets, papers, cases and all other property belonging to the library which was in his custody, for which the librarian shall give him a full receipt, discharging him from all responsibility therefor, except in the case herein provided; and on receiving the library property, the librarian shall carefully examine all books and other property appertaining to the library, and if any loss or injury shall have been sustained, for which a fine has not been imposed by his predecessor, or for which a fine has been imposed but not certified by him to the treasurer of the board of school inspectors, the librarian shall certify the amount thereof to said treasurer, who shall collect the same of such predecessor in the same manner as other fines are collected.

7. In case of vacancy in the office of librarian, the township clerk shall perform the duties of librarian until the vacancy is filled.

8. If any person, having held the office of librarian, shall neglect or refuse to deliver to his successor all the library property, as prescribed in the sixth regulation, the treasurer of the board of school inspectors shall forthwith commence an action in the name of the township for the recovery of the property he shall so neglect or refuse to deliver.

9. On the return of every book to the library, the librarian shall examine it carefully, to ascertain what injury, if any, has been sustained by it, and shall charge the amount of the fine accordingly.

10. The following fines shall be assessed by the librarian as herein provided:

First, For detaining a book beyond two weeks, five cents per week;

Second, For the loss of a volume, the cost of the book, and if one of a set an amount sufficient to purchase a new set;

Third, For a leaf of the text torn out or lost, or so soiled as to render it illegible, the cost of the book; and if one of a set the cost of a new set;

Fourth, For any injury beyond ordinary wear, an amount proportionate to the injury, to be estimated by the librarian, subject to revision, upon appeal, by the board of school inspectors;

Fifth, Whenever any book shall not be returned within six weeks from the time it was loaned, it shall be deemed to be lost, and the person so detaining it shall be charged with its cost in addition to the weekly fine for detention, up to the time such charge is made. But if the book be finally returned, the charge for loss shall be remitted; and the fine for not returning the book shall be levied up to the time of such return: *Provided*, That in no case shall the amount of weekly fines exceed double the cost of the book.

11. On the third Monday of August, November, February, and May, and also immediately before he vacates his office, the librarian shall report to the treasurer of the board of school inspectors the name of every person liable for fines, and the amount each of such persons is liable to pay; and said treasurer shall immediately proceed to collect the same, and if not paid, he shall forthwith bring an action in the name of the township for the recovery thereof.

12. The library fines collected shall first be applied to the replacing of lost volumes, binding pamphlets, and rebinding such books as may require it.

13. On the first Monday of September in each year, the librarian shall report to the township board of school inspectors as follows:

First, The number of volumes in the library;

Second, The number of volumes purchased during the year;

Third, The number of volumes presented during the year;

Fourth, The number of volumes loaned during the year [counting each volume once for each time it is loaned];

Fifth, The amount of fines assessed;

Sixth, Such other items as the board of school inspectors may require for their annual report to the superintendent of public instruction.

INDEX.

—◆—

15

www.ingramcontent.com/pod-product-compliance
Lightning Source LLC
Chambersburg PA
CBHW030553270326
41927CB00007B/907